ACTIVATE YOUR SOUL PLAN !
Angel Answers & Actions

Received and Written by
MR. PHILLIP ELTON COLLINS
THE ANGEL NEWS NETWORK

Contact: info@theangelnewsnetwork.com
ISBN: 098314334X
ISBN 13: 9780983143345

ANGEL ANSWERS AND ACTIONS

Talking to Angels Today

Whether you believe angels exist and that we can talk to them really does not matter. What matters is that we know we are loved and are capable of being loved because we came from love. If you can receive this truth, then you may support the idea that these loving forces from whence we came are still here assisting us. This concept is how humanity initially created the idea and knowledge of angels.

What matters about this book is not from where or whom the messages came, but what is being said. Even if you think I made it all up, that's OK (it's just the angel in me). Use your own resonance and discernment, your freedom of choice and will, and see if any of what is being said here can support you. Ask yourself: What is the intention of this endeavor? Is it to help or deceive? What does it feel like? True or false?

It's not necessary, but if you are able to connect with the *energy/consciousness* from a higher realm and know that what is being said in this book is in love and support of us, good for you, but again, it's not essential. **The higher-realm forces that love and support us don't need us to believe whether they exist. They are going to love and support us no matter what.**

Throughout human history, major revelations of knowledge and wisdom arrived to guide our advancement. Where did these ideas/concepts come from? Were they from a human mind? *Is there wisdom and consciousness outside the human mind that has been guiding us all along?* The great challenge for humanity is to accept that there is an intelligence outside ourselves loving and supporting us—call it angels, God, Source, ALL THERE IS.

We are all born with a divine soul plan (our purpose/reason in being here, why we came here).

All the wisdom, tools, and messages in this endeavor are intended to help you activate your soul plan. This will bring you great joy and help create a world of equality, harmony, and balance through your talents and gifts. Are you ready to activate? Here's to the angels who are helping us.

HOW TO CALL A HIGHER BEING*

To call a Higher Being
Let us first think upon them,
And in our mind's eye,
Let our seeing, become their being.

Call upon the Higher Being,
And they will answer every call
If your motive is for the good and love of all.

The Higher Being
Gives of itself unconditionally,
In all conditions, unceasingly.

Ask and ye shall receive,
If your intention is not to deceive.

For the Higher Being is here
Merely to truly please,
As you lovingly receive.

And when you meet a Higher Being,
You soon have a deep desire
To be who they are, just being.

*The poems in this book are all from *Sacred Poetry and Mystical Messages* by Phillip Elton Collins.

ACKNOWLEDGMENTS

My gratitude goes to the angelic realms that have loved and supported us, whether we know it or not. Thanks for not giving up on us. *Our not knowing them does not prevent them from being.* The angels are teaching us to love ourselves in order to create a new world of equality, harmony, and balance, and to activate our soul plans as eternal divine beings of light.

Thanks to Angel News Network social media publicist, actor, poet, playwright, and brother in all deeds, Omar Prince, who is always ready to assist in bringing spiritual messages out into the world.

Many thanks to my fellow cofounders of the Angel News Network, Jeff Fasano and Joel Anastasi, who support me in my personal process that allows the activation of my soul plan.

And to my life partner, James Gozon, who is a key component of all things possible, especially my soul plan activation.

CONTENTS

Contents

INTRODUCTION

Dear Beloved Soul Planners,
Did you know you come to Earth with a divine soul plan (your purpose in being here) within each lifetime, and it is up to you to choose or not, through your freedom of will and choice, to activate it?

This entire endeavor called *Activate Your Soul Plan! Angel Answers and Actions* is a loving tool to assist you in activating your divine soul plan. You each have been carrying your soul plan within your heart for many, many lifetimes. Sometimes you activated part of it and sometimes not. Now you are being given a unique opportunity to activate more of your soul plan than ever before through something called **ascension** (moving into a higher frequency of existence).

The answers to questions humanity has had for millennia are gifted within this endeavor, as well as a *call to action* giving you a foundation to be who you are and know why you are here. The veil of untruth has been pervasive throughout most of mankind's recorded history. It is time for us to know as much of the truth as we can comprehend. This truth will set us free from all that has kept us in lack, limitation, and duality.

Much of the truth has been forgotten or dumbed down within us for various reasons.

The guidance here offers portals and vortices to universal wisdoms to assist us in creating communities of equality, harmony, and balance; all this reflects our relationship with self. We are so much more than we ever imagined. Fear of our power and divinity has kept this knowledge from us. Now we are learning how to access our *knowing hearts* where all this knowledge is stored, so that we might gain all the wisdom we need to be the divine beings we are. Take a deep breath and connect with your heart now.

We are creations of an unlimited universe filled with ever-expanding possibilities and probabilities. It is time to regain our knowledge of who we are and to use our talents and gifts to become the master teachers and star travelers we were created to be.

We are spokes on the wheel that the universe moves upon. By expressing our truth, stating our needs, and setting our boundaries, we power this wheel. Each spoke of the wheel represents our divine soul plans activated.

Be your message each day. Create peace and joy. Do your best in each moment. As we change and heal ourselves, we shall change and heal our world, manifesting our final golden age of We Consciousness/Oneness and our immortal/eternal life.

A full range of human issues/elements is discussed within these *activation tools*. I received these teachings within a short period of time and share them with you now. Whether you read them in order or randomly, you will receive what you will need to activate your soul plan. Each chapter concludes with a poem I wrote in *Sacred Poetry and Mystical Messages*. These poems are intended to be a deeper interactivity that will also support you.

Most of all enjoy the journey; it is not just about the destination. The Light of Source never fails in supporting the activation of our soul plans.

Phillip Elton Collins

USING DISCERNMENT AND RESONANCE WITHIN OUR SPIRITUAL GROWTH

Many of us are aware that our planet and species are experiencing a shift like never before in our recorded history. Actually, shifts like we are experiencing have happened before in past golden ages. Now the old paradigm of our governments, religions, corporations, educational and medical institutions (which control us) are once again not meeting the needs of the people. We are waking to this reality and are preparing to create a new reality of equality, harmony, and balance. This will be accomplished through the activation of our soul plans.

Many of the tools and teachings to effect change are coming from higher realms, not the human mind. This is a challenge for some, but not for many others. The truth is that these higher forces have been helping move humanity for eons toward a divine destination of unity and oneness. Are we ready to accept that forces outside ourselves can and will assist us in creating a world that reflects a "universal wisdom" and allows us to move into an evolved reality? Through our discernment and resonance (how we think and feel about something, an internal gyro system) we can employ this higher support or not. There are many human teachers and messengers receiving guidance from higher realms and bringing it to us. How do you know what is true and who to trust? Let's create some guidelines that can help us.

BEING THE MESSAGE: Notice if the ones bringing higher truths to us appears to have a private and public persona that are not the same. There are those teaching one thing and being another. This deceit will no longer work in our world of fast cyber communication and transportation. Are they trying to sell you something, a remedy or workshop, at an inflated price that reflects their wounded ego?

BEING IN A PERSONAL PROCESS: It is essential that we be involved in a deep examination of the self through a process that supports our highest good. We can do this alone or with others. There are many metaphysical therapists trained to support this process. Use your discernment and resonance to find the one that feels right for you. Our personal growth is a process of inside out, not outside in. If someone tells you otherwise, use your discernment. If someone is attempting to fix you from the outside in—"take this, do that"—beware. Apply what resonates on your own.

YOUR DIVINE BIRTHRIGHT: Know in your heart that whatever is happening within you and the world is a divine process unfolding. No one else is "making" anything happen except you, being supported by higher realms (whatever you choose to call them). Our ability to grow and expand is a natural part of who we are. Awakening/remembering your divinity (not necessarily associated with any religion) is key. You are divinity expressing itself each and every moment. Look at the world around you; "we the people" are demanding our divinity and equality.

SPIRITUALITY IN THE WAY: Let us be careful that "thinking" we are spiritual is special or makes us better than anyone else. As in many human matters, spirituality can be used to say one is special and knows the true path to enlightenment. There are many paths to the same destination. We are all going to get "there"; it's just a matter of when and how we choose to learn. It's your divine right to be or to do so. Each one of us is on a unique place on our path. Accept this with compassion for self and others.

IT'S ALL ABOUT LOVE: We are all on this planet, a "LOVER-VERSITY," to learn to love self, which allows love of others. If we so choose, we can create communities of equality, harmony, and balance that support a universal cosmic love. And if we choose, we can and will create a new golden age of Oneness. What do you choose?

Allow these wisdoms within each of us to activate our soul plans.

Soulfully yours,
Phillip Elton Collins

CHAPTER 1

ARCHANGEL ACTIONS

Archangel Michael

During these extraordinary times of change on our planet and within humanity, many higher realms are "weighing in" to support our personal and planetary shifts. At this time we are focusing on angelic realms, which are joining together in love and support to assist us in creating a new reality of Unity and We Consciousness, through activating our divine soul plans. The world cannot and will not continue as the past, or we shall not survive as a species. But there is a grand plan that we do survive and move into heights of beings beyond our imagination at present. We shall now focus on one of these divine beings, Archangel Michael, with his mighty God Power sword, teaching us to move from our mind that believes to our heart that knows.

Phillip: Dearest Michael, there are so many archangels, what exactly is your focus and role?

Archangel Michael: Certain endeavors and intentions are assigned to various frequencies of consciousness. We within the Michael angelic realm largely guard and stand present to repel any and all who intend to destroy self, others, or the planet. We vibrate at a frequency of Love and Perfection for your use. Michael means "who is like God Power"; we embody the word for truth moving from the mind to the heart, allowing you to know, through a process of your choosing, who you are and why you are here. This will allow you to take responsibility for yourselves and the activation of your soul plan.

Phillip: Exactly how does your frequency achieve this?

Archangel Michael: You do, dear ones, through the integration of your I AM PRESENCE, your Divine Essence, your God Power, as you anchor more fully into your divine soul plan, the reason you are here. Then you can learn the things that are preventing this in yourself and your world. Once you know and apply this wisdom, it will be a game-changer.

Phillip: It seems you are a sort of "preventing presence."

Archangel Michael: The veil between our worlds is thinner than ever before, dear ones. This will further allow you to move more deeply in your understanding of what service the angelic realms play in your world, especially in relationship to yourself (the basis of all).

Phillip: Most people perceive you as a protector-power with your sword.

Archangel Michael: Humanity's awareness of most angels is through the concept of a guardian angel mission. So that's how most angels are in the consciousness of humanity, to a lesser or greater degree. How this expresses itself within each angelic realm has to do with the mission of each frequency. We are discussing Michael at the moment.

Phillip: So how does what you do really work?

Archangel Michael: Be careful when you call upon us, dear ones. We shall assist you in fulfilling your personal and world soul plans. Are you truly ready to do that?

Phillip: Please further explain.

Archangel Michael: It's really about the revelation of what exists within you. The "protection" comes from the God Power within you, dear ones. We merely teach you how to awaken this truth through a loving relationship with self and others.

Phillip: You're like ever-ready men.

Archangel Michael: We are ever ready to respond to your slightest call by your focusing on us. It makes no difference if you see or feel us, or believe in us. When you connect with our frequency through your emotions and thoughts or incarnational evolution, we automatically stand ready to protect and support that which is of God Power, the good of all, within you. And to assist you in healing what is preventing this.

Phillip: So we just need to focus on you?

Archangel Michael: If mankind only knew how simple this is. It's just a matter of you getting out of the way, and trusting and surrendering to our existence, and knowing we are here to assist in maintaining and sustaining all soul plans. We are not a figment of anyone's imagination, dear ones. Whenever we are given the slightest opening or recognition, we appear.

Phillip: Have you always been present in mankind's history?

Archangel Michael: Mankind, through Man Power, would have destroyed itself long ago without our constant presence. We are greater than humanity's intellect, ceaseless in our service. Fasten your seat belts; our greatest efforts are yet to come during your dispensation of ascension!

Phillip: What does that mean?

Archangel Michael: There is much change in process within yourselves and your world where only higher-realm support can be fully effective. We are here to protect all that is good. There are many shifts in your emotional, mental, and physical bodies that will affect your world. You are moving into a new age (the seventh final golden age) with new inner God Powers you do not fully understand nor know how to use. But when you are ready, all will be revealed.

Phillip: You will show us how to use these God Powers?

Archangel Michael: Yes, through the fulfillment of your divine soul plans, as you learn how to master self and existence.

Phillip: Please further explain.

Archangel Michael: You will learn the powers of self, and nature and the cosmos, as you ascend into a higher frequency of existence. You will be creating, growing, and expanding beyond your awareness now.

Phillip: As if this isn't enough, what else?

Archangel Michael: Much of our assistance will come through your healing, by love and the further activation of your I AM PRESENCE. We are the ways and means to your I AM PRESENCE and all higher realms through the healing of self and awakening your divine essence. Humanity has no idea of the inner God Power within itself. The angelic realm is connected to this ability and power within each of you. Together, there is no limit to what can be achieved—no limit to the balance of giving and receiving, dear ones.

Phillip: There is nothing in the physical world as strong as this I AM PRESENCE, is there?

Archangel Michael: Can you show us anything as strong? Can you compare anywhere what we can accomplish together without limit?

Phillip: It seems like it is time for mankind to better understand the angelic realm and how we may work together.

Archangel Michael: There are legions of us to support your fulfillment of your divine soul plans and your attainment into ascension, dear ones. You are not alone, never have been, never will be. We are here to assist in the balancing of any negative forces inside and outside you that are preventing your divine destiny from ascending back into the light. We've been doing this for eons. The time is now for blastoff.

Phillip: All we have to do is call upon you?

Archangel Michael: Yes, dear ones. Trust and surrender; we are here to assist in preventing anything less than perfect coming forth. Our sword of truth will cut through this. Any doubt will prevent this.

Phillip: What is the biggest prevention now?

Archangel Michael: Mankind must become conscious and desire to receive the God Power within itself. War does not work and cannot continue; honor yourself and others, your planet. You need to reconnect with the higher realms from which you came; all lack and limitation and suffering you have created will end. Can you simply trust and surrender and come to us? We are all-powerful and wish only to spread our blessings upon you. Can you receive them now? We shall answer every heartfelt call and assist in the fulfillment of each soul plan. This is how much we love you. Now love yourselves enough to receive our giving.

Phillip: Thank you with all my heart.

CHAPTER 2

CALL UPON HIGHER REALMS REGULARLY

As the elements continue to shift and change in our relationship with self, others, and the outer world, let us continue to call upon higher God Power realms for love and support. In this endeavor, the realms of angels assisting us to activate our soul plans are our priority.

Humanity has largely lost contact with these ancient, God-powerful, and protecting forces that have always been with us. We have never been alone. These energies can and will infuse self and the environment with support/wisdom, much stronger than anything in our frequency, to help eliminate any imbalances in the human self in order to create a new world of equality, harmony, and balance.

More than ever before, let us call upon these higher realms to allow them to offer support in our building a new civilization reflecting a permanent We Consciousness of Unity and Oneness. The time has come to move from the "me" to the "we," and for humanity to move into full activation of individual soul plans. The shocking reality is that if mankind continues to be left to its own devices, our destructive desires within us are capable of destroying the planet and ourselves. It has happened before.

These Man Power forces are insane, and the support of the higher God Power realms is essential, and can and will assist us in awakening our inner Divine Essence to save us from ourselves. It is time to establish a new pattern reconnecting us to our innate goodness through these higher realms and have it reflect out to the many. Then we can become the custodians of boundless oneness, God Power, abundance, cosmic intelligence…boundless everything. Are you ready?

The balance and action of our emotions and thoughts will allow a new world to unfold. Through the higher-realm teachings, we can become fully conscious of any imbalances in our emotions and thoughts that do not support the highest good of self and others. The Angel News Network and many, many other outlets are dedicated to such teachings.

There is much mischief in our emotions and thoughts that has caused us to give our God Power away to others in religion, government, corporations, etc. We can set ourselves free from what we have housed within us by calling upon the invincible higher realms' ever-present support. Mankind has held itself prisoner far too long. These mighty forces can teach us how to process ourselves into freedom.

Remember, when we call upon higher realms: (1) negative Man Power forces cannot affect higher realms, (2) negative forces are consumed by the positive, and (3) negative forces know the higher realms mean their annihilation. Energy always entrains to the highest frequency; every positive has an electronic force field that attracts a like kind. Higher realms have the ability to control any amount of energy and keep it from lower/denser energy.

When, through our freedom of will and choice, will we have the courage to choose a higher frequency of existence? These higher God Power realm energies are greater than the humanity of this world. It is our destiny to embody them and annihilate anything other than the highest good of self and all.

Let us maintain and sustain the inner God Power within each of us, ever growing and expanding into the mission of creating the seventh final golden age of Oneness/We Consciousness.

Allow our destiny now to clear and cleanse all the negative emotions and thoughts of the past and present. If not now, when, dear brothers and sisters, are we going to demand and command ourselves, our world, into our birthright of God Power Oneness? This can only be done with the unconditional, loving support of higher realms—ever ready, ever present.

Then we shall be victorious in embracing and embodying the divine soul plan of self and planet to become the higher realms that guide and support us. Let us go forward and feel the presence of these divine beings who love us more than we can love ourselves right now; to free ourselves from further suffering through becoming our higher selves and joining the higher realms in Oneness. Now is the crucial time to activate our soul plans with the assistance of angels.

CHAPTER 3

A DIVINE DESTINATION: YOUR DIVINITY

From the Great White Brotherhood

Dear Sisters and Brothers,

All of your lifetimes lead to the same destination (how and when you get there are your choices): the eternal connection to your divinity. *You need not believe this; it does not matter.* For you will come to this truth on your own when you are ready, through your freedom of will and choice.

You will reach your *divine destination* when you have learned all you need to learn by not knowing it. One of your favorite learning tools is learning "what is" through "what is not." You have eons of examples of this. There are easier ways to learn, but this seems to be the one most of you prefer and need.

Your judgment, shaming, blaming, duality, separation, and confrontation are some of your favorite dense-frequency tools to the divine destination of which we speak. Dear ones, there is no right or wrong, or good or bad, to the process: **it** simply **"is."** These are all aspects of the same thing. Darkness allows you to know there is light.

When you reach your divine destination (your direct connection to ALL THERE IS) only you need to know and accept and welcome your arrival.

Dear ones, all your lives on this planet have been a *constant beginning, not an end.* Your extended purpose in being will grow and expand when you set yourself free from the dense frequency where you currently reside *to become the master teachers of the universe.* (The reason you signed on to all this!) The most essential tools in gaining your freedom are your resonance and discernment. These will show you your UNIQUE PATH to your *destination of divinity.*

As you have heard many times before, the universe would be incomplete without each and every one of you (this includes the minerals, plants, and animals, as well). Can you receive this truth now? Take a deep breath and receive some more of this truth now.

None of your journey is about real or unreal, seen or unseen, or knowledge; *it is about truth and wisdom (collected over many lifetimes). Wisdom is truth reflecting the Cosmic Law of Love—that being you and God Power.*

Love and truth are inseparable, eternal, and unchanging. These can be known but not changed. Love and truth are the essential aspects of ALL THERE IS; they are beyond teaching and time. They can be best found within and through a personal process examination of yourself. (See Life Mastery, www.theangelnewsnetwork.com.)

Dear ones, your journey has no beginning, it has no end. IT SIMPLY IS a choice you made in

agreeing to be human, experiencing all aspects of humanity being God. In reality, none of your 3-D life path can exist apart from the higher realms from whence it originated.

Your 3-D world is composed of beliefs in opposites and separate wills, often leading to confrontation. Look at your world right now. **This world leads to constant resistance since it is not really who you are.**

The good news is that you are in the process of waking up and knowing your life and world have been illusions you created in order to learn from it and to leave it. It's all been a "Lover-versity." **The world you have created is merely a reflection of your internal relationship with yourself based upon a lack of love.** Since love is the building block of *ALL THERE IS*, *and ALL THERE IS* is all there is, it can ask for nothing else.

As you continue to wake up from your 3-D illusion by accepting with compassion and forgiving why you created it all, you can choose **forgiveness**. Through forgiveness you can remember who you are and why you are here by releasing/graduating yourself from the **cosmic classroom you created** to now know the truth.

You are God experiencing itself in all ways in order to master density and to release yourself from it, in order to enter and be in service to ALL THERE IS. Remember always, this will allow you to become the master teachers of the universe, your purpose in being here.

Now you are remembering, for what we have just said is all stored in your heart. Access your heart, dear ones, when you forget again. It is all eternally stored there.

OUR TRUE STATE OF BEING

In reality formless best describes
Our true state of beingness.

Right now I am housing my formlessness,
In a human body,
But oddly enough
I am almost ready to set that form
Aside and ride away
And decide another day,
If I'll come this way, again.

One's form serves only a brief respite
While relates to the journey
One supports,
In a particular point in time,
And port.

No matter what form I choose,
I can never really lose

CHAPTER 4

ASCENDING ASCENSION

From Archangel Uriel, World Teacher and Guardian

D ear Beloved Light Beings on Earth,
    When you look up into your night sky and you see celestial bodies radiating light, not reflecting light, know that each one of them went through an ascension process very much like what you are going through now. **You are born from the light and you return to the light**, dear ones. Each planet returning to being a star (body of light) has its own unique soul plan, just like you. The *planet phase* is the way the process of ascension can take place; the destination is the light. There is no other way to be; this is **creation in action**. What happens in between light to light is your sacred journey of returning to your divinity, being in service to ALL THERE IS. Once you return to the light, you can decide what you create from the light again; it is endless and limitless. **This is the way the universe keeps eternally growing and expanding.**

Each planet, solar system, galaxy, and universe is born and expands this way. There are different frequencies of intention for each of these. **Your purpose and intention is to learn to master love**, since love is the foundation of all creation. Everything else is the absence of love. You have experienced a lot of nonlove to now know love. *You are learning "what is" through "what is not."* This is not the easiest path to wisdom, but the one you chose, *the contract to which you agreed.* That contract is coming to maturation and expiration, dear ones.

It is time for you to know how **to become multidimensional**, and connect and even travel within higher realms of this solar system, galaxy, and beyond. **It is time to bridge the separation between dense matter and light**. As your planet aspires to become a star, as you the light being who will inhabit the star, all questions will be answered; you will know your divine nature and your Oneness with ALL THERE IS. Once you gain this connection, there will be no desire or need to be physical, have things, and work for money; abundance will be your eternity. **Your pursuits will be of a higher nature in service to the forces of Creation**. You have been preparing for this ever since you came to this planet from other worlds.

You did not evolve here; you are an essential part of this ascension process on this particular planet and in this solar system and galaxy.

Let us further discuss your divine light nature and begin to experience the Oneness of ALL THERE IS. Take a deep breath, dear ones; **connect with your heart space** that already knows all of which we speak, and *allow your heart to speak to you now.*

This is your heart speaking directly to you; listen and learn:

* All you have agreed to experience has been a pathway awakening your consciousness to knowing you were created by love and are love.

* When your Earth journey is complete, your star journey begins, as a being of light.

* Once you are a star being (again), your service to ALL THERE IS really begins, as your world service ends.

* Your eternal soul to spirit being will guide you back to your true home.

* All time and distance will end, and your new life will have no beginning or end.

* Elements of light are your nutrients now powering you homeward.

* Ancient memories and wisdom are coming into your consciousness, along with how to apply them.

* You are experiencing Oneness/We Consciousness. You have never felt such belonging.

* Emotions and thoughts seem not to matter now; the vibrations of the celestial spheres are replacing them.

* Language that you have known will not be necessary as you telepathically know and communicate with all.

* Connecting to ALL THERE IS transitions into the infinite now.

* Bliss, peace, and joy are your primary experiences.

* Sound and color speak to you softly and lead you forward beyond the beyond.

* Cosmic unconditional love warms your beingness.

* You are formless, eternal light.

* You know your God Power, which always was, is ever present now.

* Eternity celebrates your presence, and you know why you experience all that has preceded this moment.

* Like never before, you know who you are and why you are here.

* Oneness becomes all that matters, in the absence of matter, offering limitless expansion.

* Your state of being has merged with ALL THERE IS.

* The timelessness and physical nonbeingness powers you further into limitless potential.

* Your human self has found its true ownership, a divine temple of ever-present ALL THERE IS.

* Your consciousness/awareness has become truly divine as it morphs further into your star beingness.

* The light is your pathway, surrounded by divine direction.

* Your total being expands before you.

* Your heart has known all this throughout every life you ever had.

Now you know why so many of you signed on to the ascension train: an amazing journey not to be missed or repeated again.

HOW TO BE AN ASCENDED MASTER, FASTER

The creative life forces within our bodies
Are to be raised into
The crown of your head,

And instead of flowing down,
Are to flow up in recognition, instead,
Of your I AM Presence,
Which is always around.

Then through awakened oneness,
Thoughts and emotions,
Needing nothing else,
We can conceive creative works
At the mental and emotional levels
Through the creation of equality,
Harmony and balance,
With the alliance of
Idealistic ideas, ideals of art,
Imagination and invention,
That serves and blesses,
All our intention.

With this constructive consciousness
The physical body can remain,
Eternally youthful and beautiful
Being the image and likeness,
And brightness of the God-likeness, within.

Once we achieve immortality,
And creator consciousness,
Our true mission begins,
As the ascended master, faster,
Mending the past, we awaken at last,
And feel the good God-force, again.

Feeling gloriously connected
To perfection and true direction
Our true divine soul plan, begins...

CHAPTER 5

BEING MULTIDIMENSIONAL

Received from the Council of Archangelic Realms (CAR)

Dear Beloved Humans-Beings,

As your spiritual DNA and higher chakras are now being activated once again through a process you call ASCENSION, it is time, if you so choose, to once again directly connect with the higher frequency/vibrational realms from whence you came and who maintain and sustain you at present.

What your scientists have called your "junk" DNA, which is your true energetic connection to your higher self, is now allowing the reactivations of your eight through twelve chakras (above your present one through seven), which coordinate with the twelve star systems that seeded your planet. Not to overload you with too much star data at this time, please know each star system brings a monadic priority to the diversity within your planet's and humanity's soul plans. There is no planet in the universe with your diversity of star systems. **You are a divine experiment of diversity learning to love itself.**

Your higher DNA and chakras were originally deactivated from past abuse and disconnection to higher realms. Now you are being given the opportunity to permanently reconnect to higher realms to manifest your final golden age.

What all this growth and expansion with your DNA and chakras means is that you are reconnecting with dimensions/realms above and beyond where you mostly reside now. There are many light workers and way showers **showing the way by being their message and allowing higher-realm connections/guidance.** There is nothing special about anyone connecting with (channeling) higher realms at this time. If they say so, or insist they are the true, one, and only path to truth, use your own resonance and discernment to move away from them.

Master teachers do not call themselves "masters"; they simply re-create themselves! Be cautious of anyone who asks you to follow or worship the guru. Your higher selves reside within you and are patiently waiting for your awakening, dear ones.

Your ascension process has always been and always will be a process of inside out (not outside in) through your freedom of choice and will. You'll all eventually get there; it's just a matter of when and how.

Each of you has "fragments" within your soul plans, which will allow you to resonate with specific higher frequencies as essential aspects of your soul plan. You will each receive/connect with the frequency/consciousness that best serves your highest good and needs. **This is a divine union that only you can choose, or not. Once you choose, you are chosen, dear ones!**

Beware, dear ones, your mental body or others may attempt to sabotage the entire process by telling you, you are not good enough or worthy enough to receive such a connection, or others may tell you this goes against all established beliefs and truths. Well, a belief from the mental body often changes, and truth only lives within your knowing hearts (not outside yourself).

Take another deep breath, dear ones. Release yourself from yourself and know what you are about to receive is not about you, dear ones. Allow yourself to become connected to another multidimensional aspect of itself and become a vessel of it. **You are finally realizing you're here to be in world service to one another and Source/Creation/ God. This service can only be achieved from your divine self-love reflecting out.**

Dear ones, all your so-called inventions and advancements as a species were/are the result of the higher-realm connections of which we speak now. Your brains simply received; they did not create! It is the unconditional love of the higher realms that makes all of this possible.

So take another deep breath, dear ones, and begin to know and realize who you truly are as multidimensional beings having this human experience, and begin to accept with compassion that true wisdom (not knowledge) comes from the higher realms you are beginning to accept as an essential aspect of self.

You are more glorious and amazing than your minds can ever imagine right now, dear ones. Once you truly know this, you will *create a world that reflects this truth*, and then your real work begins.

TAKING OUR POWER BACK

Once upon a time through
The abuse of our power
We lost our power
In order to regain it in a new hour,
Now.

We were connected to
ALL THERE IS,
But that wasn't enough.
Through freedom of will and choice
We thought our minds
Could make a better choice.

For eons in our "mind field,"
We've learned a lot about,
What is,
Through what is not.

Now the mind is returning
To the heart,
And we are ready,
To start a new start.
Let us re-connect,
And correct and connect,
To ALL THERE IS, in effect.

Only through a renewed true connect
Can we correct our forgetfulness,
And create heartfelt consciousness.

Once awake,
We shall remember,
Who we are,
Why we are here,
And take our power back,
And never throw it back,
As true divine beings.

CHAPTER 6

COUNCIL OF ARCHANGELIC REALMS (CAR)

Excerpt from Divine Discussions Channeled
By the Author with Joel Anastasi

Greetings Brethren of Humanity,

On this day you are remembering the importance of love. You are remembering that the mission of the planet that you have incarnated on multiple times is to learn to love.

We are the Council of the Archangelic Realms coming to you at this time, representing many realms of archangelic forces, if you will. Today we shall spearhead, as you might say, the energies of Gabriel, Michael, Raphael, and Uriel.

Why do we do this, dear one? Why do we focus on the day of the heart on four major archangelic forces, realms, and bands of consciousness whose mission—whose responsibility, if you will—is to serve humanity? For the questions that linger in your hearts and minds at this time, with the endeavor you call the Angel News Network, is to define through your heart spaces what is the connection to these forces, of which we are administrators, in combination with the mission you call the Angel News Network. Is that not what you're pondering, dear brother and dear ones? Indeed it is.

Through your studies, and through the activation of the fragments of each of your soul plans, the brethren of the Angel News Network have connected with various frequencies of the archangelic realms and other higher realms—beyond, beneath, above, and below the archangelic realms—within your individual and collective endeavors, have you not, dear ones?

So at this time we would like to assist you in amalgamating and integrating, if you so choose, the missions of each of these particular frequencies—Gabriel, Michael, Raphael, and Uriel—and how they integrate with individual soul plans and the mission to bring higher realms to humanity, dear ones. For that is what you have chosen, is it not—that you will be the messengers of higher realms in this particular discussion, the frequencies of archangelic energies and teachings, to free humanity from yourself.

For that is the task, the mission at hand. Is humanity ready to transcend the density of humanity and transmute into its ascended higher frequency? Not to eliminate humanity, but simply to allow it to go into its true eternal—immortal, if you will—formatting. So as you have experienced directly with these realms and studied on your own, each of these frequencies has a particular mission, which you are familiar with and are becoming more familiar with as you integrate, amalgamate, and connect with these frequencies as an organic grace and ease process that all of humanity is in the process of achieving, dear ones.

For it is your divine destiny to connect with higher realms; to become telepathic, if you will, with us on a new normal basis so that you will become permanently connected to our frequencies and others like us in order to facilitate your final golden age on this planet. And why is that, dear ones? As many of you know, it is the time for your planet—your home, Mother Earth, Gaia—to return to a being of light. The cosmic cycle is taking place of returning to the energy and the light from which you came. Thus, in turn, as the planet returns to a conscious living being of light, all those elementals—minerals, plants, animals, and humanity within and upon the body of light—in order to maintain and sustain existence, will be light as well. Quite simple.

So we realize you have questions about individuated involvements and connections with archangelic frequencies; how that relates to individual soul plans and the collective soul plans of your mission to bring higher-realm messages, and thus increase the resonance and consciousness of humanity to amalgamate and integrate with the increased vibration and frequency of the planet, which has chosen to ascend—transmute, if you will—into light.

We have the capacity at this time to connect with each of the frequencies of Gabriel, Michael, Raphael, and Uriel, whose frequencies are with us now as a Council of Archangelic Realms, realizing that your connection and the connection of the channel whom we come through at this time will be your own unique connection with each one of those frequencies.

So we ask you not to compare your connection with anyone else's connection, realizing that your connection will be in concert with your soul plan and with the soul plan of that particular higher realm. How may we assist you, dear one?

Joel: Thank you so much for joining us. I feel very honored.

Council: The honor is ours, dear one. It is we who are in service to you, dear one.

Joel: Thank you. I guess we're really in service to each other. I guess I'm just beginning to understand more fully what you just said about our individual connections to each one of those energies known as the archangelic realms. I'd like to start with me.

Council: Always a good place to start, dear one.

Joel: I told the council that I felt most connected to the Gabriel realm and asked what my mission with that energy might be, and what I could do to engage it more fully.

Council: Yes, it is a process of your soul plan to choose through your resonance and then to be chosen. That is the giving and receiving of the process that you call channeling. So we would ask you to know that you are already in service through the work that you have done and the work that you are doing. In effect, you are asking yourself, am I ready to grow and expand beyond where I have been to somewhere else? Is that not true, dear one?

So what are the components within that process that are taking place? The process that you are currently teaching is knowing that you are good enough; that you are worthy enough to be this, to choose this, to no longer completely have to depend on the information of higher realms coming through others—although not eliminating that, by all means—but at the same time realizing that there is a fragment in your soul plan that you wish to express through your talents and gifts directly, without that process coming through someone else.

So what would you think it would take within yourself—to know through your heart, to move your belief through knowing—for this process you're asking about to take place, dear one?

Joel: I know it already.

Council: And what do you know, dear one?

Joel: That I am ready, that I have the ability. Robert and Jeff began suddenly. I've gone through a longer period of preparation than they did.

Council: There is no need to compare one to the other, dear one.

Joel: I guess I'm reassuring myself that I am prepared. How much more do I need to be prepared?

Council: What does that reflect, "having to prepare yourself," dear one?

Joel: The sense of not being good enough, not loving myself enough.

Council: So if we were to identify, in concert with you, one core issue that may have presented itself in the past and into the present and future, what might that be?

Joel: Loving myself enough to realize that I'm good enough and worthy enough.

Council: Yes, dear one. And through the process of being that direct receiver—call it what you will, this particular frequency of Gabriel—let us now connect with the frequency of Gabriel itself, shall we?

Joel: Yes, wonderful.

Gabriel: Greetings, beloved scribe. We of Gabriel are with you now. For many, many of your Earth years we have been interfacing, have we not, dear one?

Joel: If you say so.

Gabriel: What do you say, dear one?

Joel: I believe everything Gabriel says. I accept that, yes.

Gabriel: What exactly has been taking place in the interaction of you and we of Gabriel over the years, dear one? What was it about this particular frequency with which you resonated?

Joel: The power of the wisdom. The power of the wisdom was so overwhelming to help mankind know who they are and why they are here.

Gabriel: Yes, wisdom beyond knowledge, for knowledge does not necessarily contain wisdom, which your planet and your world have been experiencing. So it was the resonance, the attraction to wisdom, dear one?

Joel: Yes, and the power of the love that it was expressing.

Gabriel: Yes, it is that unconditional love, that cosmic unconditional love of all the archangelic forces—we, one of many who serve humanity and serve source—that you feel. So here we stand face-to-face, dear one. Face-to-face, Gabriel and yourself. Face-to-face in this moment of now, asking the question, how shall we expand our connection, our communication, dear one?

Joel: Yes, that is the question.

Gabriel: And what do you choose, dear one?

Joel: I choose to expand our connection.

Gabriel: In what way, dear one?

Joel: To open myself and get myself out of the way. That is the best I know how to answer that question.

Gabriel: Yes, dear one, to quiet that fervent mental body. That mental body that has often prevented what you now say you yearn to express within yourself in connection to us, because the connection to us, if that is what you so choose, is merely a nutrient for your soul. If it feeds and nourishes your soul authentically and transparently, dear one, it will feed nutrients to others. What aspect of yourself will our aspect nourish, dear one?

Joel: My heart.

Gabriel: Yes, dear one. What within your knowing heart, dear one?

Joel: It will nourish the knowing that I am God functioning as God.

Gabriel: What are the aspects of living that you love the most?

Joel: The beauty, the joy, all the gorgeous creations of God, the music, everything that lifts my heart with joy.

Gabriel: Anything else, dear one?

Joel: Is this a test? [*Laughs.*]

Gabriel: There are no tests, dear one, as your educational systems are beginning to learn. What is a passion of yours, dear one, which we, in connection with you, often fulfilled, and brings you joy and ease by bringing it out into your world? What is that?

Joel: It's the understanding and meaning that we are God and we are all connected.

Gabriel: And what is that?

Joel: It is God. It helps me know God. It helps me know love.

Gabriel: What are we of Gabriel attempting for you to uncover within yourself that is so deep, that is so ancient within yourself?

Joel: That I am God expressing. That is the best I know how to answer that.

Gabriel: Dear one, it is truth.

Joel: Well, OK, that's God expressing. Isn't that truth?

Gabriel: It is truth, dear one. Does that resonate?

Joel: Absolutely. That's what knocked me out the first time I heard you coming through Robert. It drew me to you like a magnet.

Gabriel: And we had to do this roundabout to get to it, dear one. So we want to take a moment, now that we have revealed and uncovered that, to say that it is not some deep, dark secret within self. It is that *passion* within you.

Joel: To reveal the truth.

Gabriel: Yes, dear one.

Joel: Absolutely.

Gabriel: That's it, truth. Say it, dear one.

Joel: Truth! Truth! Truth!

Gabriel: You know in your heart what this frequency represents when it comes to the structures, the endeavors, the aspirations of humanity; the foibles that have and are continuing to take place. It is the buoyant passion and fragment in your soul plan of truth that will set you and humanity free, is it not, dear one?

Joel: It is, absolutely. That is what *The Second Coming* is all about. That's why I asked all those questions about what was going on in our world, so that the truth would be revealed through the wisdom of the divine realms.

Gabriel: *The Second Coming* is truth, dear one, is it not?

Joel: Yes, it's a gorgeous, powerful book.

Gabriel: So, this is our observation. In your questioning mind, when you doubt that you are good enough or worthy enough to make this connection, we ask you, through your heart, to connect with the *passion of truth* and know exactly how essential that is, and who you are and why you are here, dear one.

Joel: That is helpful, thank you. It's interesting how Robert and Jeff seemed to begin their channeling by simply appearing to be suddenly knocked out, and then they began channeling the messages of Gabriel and Michael.

Gabriel: Dear one, it was not quite that simple. That may be what you or others observed, but there were multiple incarnational cycles to prepare for that moment of being "knocked out," if you will, and receiving that message. What you may not be aware of is they had inclinations and invitations repeatedly, even in this incarnational cycle, which they closed the door to, as the channel we are coming through now has done multiple times before with the Archangelic Realm of Uriel and other frequencies. We knocked, knocked, knocked on their doors and sometimes they literally had to be knocked out.

Joel: Were you knocking on my door?

Gabriel: What do you think?

Joel: I guess you were. You must have been knocking on my door.

Gabriel: Dear one, we ask you to go back to that moment, which you have shared so often with others, when you had the first connection with us through the divine soul through whom we first came to you. That's the first knock, dear one. Can you remember?

Joel: Yes, I was knocked out! [*Laughs.*] I had to return to Robert's sessions.

Gabriel: Knock, knock! Who's there? Can you listen and answer the question now? Knock, knock, who's there?

Joel: Joel. Joel is there. Joel.

Gabriel: And who's Joel?

Joel: Joel is a divine soul.

Gabriel: What else?

Joel: Joel is a scribe for Gabriel.

Gabriel: What else, dear one?

Joel: Joel is a receiver of truth.

Gabriel: Ah, that word, truth, again. We had to dig for it a little. There it is.

Joel: I was able to have conversations with Gabriel. Robert couldn't, maybe internally.

Gabriel: Oh, that channel had many conversations with us. Yes, dear one. He is with us now, dear one.

Joel: Is he? It's so good to hear that. Can we work together in some way?

Gabriel: Would you like to rephrase that?

Joel [*laughing*]: So we're going to be working together!

Gabriel: Even more affirmative, dear one?

Joel: We **ARE** working together!

Gabriel: Hmmm. How does that feel?

Joel: Oh, God, it feels wonderful!

Gabriel: Allow that feeling to *empower* you, dear one. That's the purpose of emotions and feelings for humanity. Now you're beginning to see the tool of emotion.

Joel: In all honesty, I have been feeling that Ron Baker has picked up the mantle. There are beautiful messages coming through Ron from Gabriel. But you have already addressed the fact that we should not compare our experience to another's.

Gabriel: Dear one, neither of you will be the only connection to this frequency. There are many among you.

Joel: So you are counseling me to get out of the way, relax into it, feel it, and allow it. I guess it will be through automatic writing?

Gabriel: What do you see as your largest obstacle, dear one?

Joel: Me.

Gabriel: What aspect of me?

Joel: Not believing that it is so.

Gabriel: Where does the belief reside?

Joel: In my mind.

Gabriel: Ah, the mind, that thing.

Joel: I have to be in my heart.

Gabriel: Allow the mind to observe the heart. What was your other question, dear one?

Joel: About the automatic writing.

Gabriel: You're asking the format?

Joel: Yes.

Gabriel: That is the mental body, dear one, wanting to know how. Allow the process to take place, whether it is handwritten, electronic, or telepathic. The channel we are working through now is working in multiple forms of human communication, almost every form there is. Don't limit yourself. Just allow it to come, which feels resonant to you. Do not label it.

Joel: Michael has taught us, let your path forward be guided by joy and ease. I would love to be able to talk and record the wisdom coming through, just relax into it and let it come forth.

Gabriel: Coming through whom, dear one?

Joel: Through me.

Gabriel: Oh, and what do you think would prevent that, dear one?

Joel: Me. What else could it be but me? I guess my thinking is that we have different gifts, and the Marys have pointed out that my gift is automatic writing. They have never suggested that it is limited to that. But that is what I normally think of as being my gift. But that is laborious and tedious.

Gabriel: And it is limiting, dear one.

Joel: It is limiting. I would love to be able to speak the messages the way Phillip does, and Jeff and Robert have.

Gabriel: Oh, say the sentence you just said again, dear one.

Joel: I would love to speak the messages the way Robert and Jeff and Phillip do.

Gabriel: How may you, from the impeccability of the word, make that more of an affirmation?

Joel: I am speaking the wisdom of Gabriel, as a channel of Gabriel. That felt good.

Gabriel: Can you take ownership of that?

Joel: Yes, I can and I am. I am. You're really helping me a lot. You know that, don't you?

Gabriel: Oh, we're pretty good at that.

Joel [*laughing*]: I love to be able to chuckle with Gabriel, which I don't find happening very much with Michael.

Gabriel: Well, that sword is a heavy load, dear one.

Joel [*laughing*]: Your trumpet isn't so heavy?

Gabriel: Oh, you get to blow some hot air through it, dear one. It lightens the load.

Joel: Well, I seek to help lighten the load of people who have become so serious. We're all so serious.

Gabriel: Levity can be a wonderful integration point of wisdom, can it not?

Joel: Indeed. I can use a little more levity in my classes, which are feeling a little strenuous right now. I'd like to ask you about the Angel News Network, the ANN. I feel as though we have laid the foundation, and I realize we should just let it unfold, but it would be nice to get some insights and perspectives from your realm about where we, the men who created ANN, are going as an organization.

Gabriel: What would you say is taking place at this moment? What was the message of the Council of Archangelic Realms recently to you, dear one? Was it heard?

Joel: Yes, thank you.

Gabriel: Was it heard, dear one?

Joel: Probably not well enough by me.

Gabriel: Perhaps you will listen now, dear one. Does that answer your question?

Joel: Yes, it does. I would like to play an expanded role in all that.

Gabriel: I would *like?*

Joel: I *intend* to play an expanded role. Thank you. Impeccability of the word.

Gabriel: Oh, yes, an ancient lesson humanity loves to skate-board around.

Joel: This has been wonderful. Is there anything more you would like to say to me?

Gabriel: Only if you have need. We could go on forever, dear one.

Joel: I have to take responsibility for myself, and I hear what you're saying. So I am taking responsibility for myself, which is the lesson we've just covered in my Life Mastery class.

Gabriel: Ah, are we teaching what we need to learn, dear one?

Joel: Is that possible, do you think? [*Laughs.*]

Gabriel: We can't imagine, dear one. We simply can't.

Joel: Do you have a word for Omar?

Gabriel: Dear one, we should switch to the frequency of Raphael for this divine soul.

Joel: That would be wonderful. Thank you, Gabriel.

Gabriel: You are welcome, dear one. We are always with you.

Raphael: Greetings from the Archangelic Realm of Raphael. How may we assist you, dear one?

Joel: Can I make a little joke?

Raphael: Go for it, dear one.

Joel: It feels a little bit like musical archangels [*laughs*], moving from archangel to archangel.

Raphael: There you go. Run with it, dear one.

Joel: Thank you so much. The messages that have been coming through Omar already are exquisite. I was wondering if you had a word for beloved Omar.

Raphael: We would like to say the same thing that Gabriel, Michael, and Uriel have recently reminded you of, dear one. As receivers of specific frequencies—in this case, the Archangelic Realm of Raphael—each individual is healing what he/she needs to heal through receiving the resonance, vibration, and frequency of this particular band of consciousness within self. The divine soul of which you speak has reached a point in his processing and in his path being human of finally ratcheting up, if you will, to receive a higher level of vibration and frequency to assist in the completion of the healing of wounds and defenses as a result of the maturation and the incarnational cycles on this planet. Does this help you?

Joel: I think Omar is recognizing his worthiness and recognizing that he's capable of doing something that he is not quite believing at this point.

Raphael: And using, dear one, his talents and gifts through the expression of this particular frequency you call Raphael that you are experiencing, are you not?

Joel: Yes, that's absolutely true. It has a lyricism that the other channeling doesn't quite have, and I think that reflects his gifts and talents.

Raphael: Indeed, dear one.

Joel: So it is truly beautiful. It's the wisdom plus the style.

Raphael: What is essential is this divine soul sees this beauty and this wisdom, and being able to accept that himself, dear one.

Joel: Raphael, we haven't had the blessing of your wisdom nearly as much as we have had Michael and some of the other entities. We certainly welcome it, and thank you for joining us more fully through Omar.

Raphael: Pay attention to the synchronicity of it happening within your endeavor and your mission and frequency you have brought out into the world proclaiming and declaring and now, perhaps, demanding and commanding your mission to bring these frequencies of higher realms to the world to assist humanity in raising its vibration, thus its consciousness, dear one.

Joel: The demanding and the commanding part, I do understand that. But that is challenging for me to recognize that.

Raphael: And why would you think that so, dear one?

Joel: Obviously because we've seen ourselves as lowly human beings, not expressions of God, so the idea that we could command messengers of God, the archangelic realms! WHAT? [*Laughs.*]

Raphael: We cannot act otherwise, dear one. We cannot assist you without your permission, and your asking or your demanding or your commanding.

Joel: What would be a demonstration of demanding and commanding that the archangelic realms would respond to?

Raphael: Simply say it.

Joel: I command and demand the Archangelic Realm of Gabriel to work with me and through me?

Raphael: How does that make you feel, dear one?

Joel: Powerful. But I don't want to offend anybody. [*Laughs.*]

Raphael: Who would you offend, since we cannot be offended, dear one?

Joel: Well, I guess it's just an illusion.

Raphael: You would just offend yourself, dear one.

Joel: I can become comfortable with that quickly. It's just a matter of allowing myself to become used to it.

Raphael: You will not be forcing yourself, dear one. You will be amalgamating it.

Joel: I really feel that I am prepared to bring forth the wisdom and truth of the Gabriel realm. I think I have earned it. I've worked hard to earn it.

Raphael: Suppose we were to say it is simply your destiny. You didn't have to work for it, dear one. You didn't have it earn it. It simply just had to be. Allowing it to be in a state of beingness will allow your doingness.

Joel: Yes, I can accept all that. From the human perspective, I would say that all my work has contributed to my ability to be.

Raphael: Are you complete, dear one?

Joel: I am. Thank you so much, Raphael, for coming to us.

Raphael: You're very welcome, dear one.

Council: We're now back with the Council of Archangelic Realms and we bid you adieu. We fill our hearts with gratitude for the connection we are making with your endeavor and the endeavors of many others at this time, dear ones. Know we are here to be in service to humanity through you and with you.

THE MYTH OF DUALITY

Duality is a myth!
A taught, learned condition
Which has kept us miffed, for eons.

When we raise our consciousness to oneness
This illusion of life
Becomes noneness.

Moving from the me to the we awareness
Spares us the continued pain
Which we no longer need to maintain and sustain.

Have not we learned all we need to learn
From separation, isolation and confrontation?

The truth is, the myth of duality
No longer needs to exist,
Nor persist.

CHAPTER 7

CODES OF ANGELIC ACCESS

From the Council of Archangelic Realms (CAR)

Dear Beloved Humans of whom we are in service,
      In order to further access and assimilate the many teachings of the various angelic realms in service to humanity, we would like to present the Codes of Angelic Access:

* Being balanced within your emotional, mental, and physical bodies is always essential when you are attempting to access something new and true. Any imbalances prevent your ability to integrate wisdom (not knowledge). Endeavors such as the Angel News Network have directly received from us multiple angelic teachings to assist you in your personal and planetary processes. (A library of books, archives of video/audio channelings, the Life Mastery program, oaths of the light worker/ way shower, five agreements, six sacred messages, etc.)

*   Being open to the truth that there is something vaster and wiser than the human mind. The human mind just may be a "receiver," not an originator of information in your advancement as a species.

*   Knowing that you are love and lovable, and capable of receiving and giving love equally.

*   Stand strong within your truth, needs, and boundaries as divine spiritual beings having this human experience. Know that there are higher realms here to support and love you.

*   There really isn't a "right" and a "wrong"; these often change and can produce duality and separation. Use your resonance and discernment (your internal gyro system) to determine what works for you.

*   Beliefs come from the mind and change all the time; wisdom (accumulated knowledge) comes from the knowing heart. Learn to "think" with your heart as you create a new paradigm of oneness. Allow your useful mind to return in service to your heart.

*   The altered ego housed in your mental body is often the home of your self-sabotage. Thank the ego for sharing, but tell it to shut up. Your ego wishes you to stay within your comfort zones of the familiar. Your emotions, not in agreement with your mental body, just may be saying, "Fly."

* All of you are here for a unique reason (soul plan), knowing the universe would be incomplete without each of you. You are here to access your soul plan and purpose in learning to love. Your individuated gifts and talents are present to serve the world's soul plan and shift things into a higher frequency of reality.

* The process of raising your awareness/consciousness is not a straight line forward; be accepting, compassionate, and forgiving for whatever your process is. Try not to compare it to anyone else's.

* Allow joy and bliss to be your indicators of being on your true path. Grace and ease are good signs of being true to your purpose in being here. You are not here to suffer or to be punished; these are distortions of the human mind's need to control.

* You are stewards of your planet, all things within and upon it, self, and one another. Know that all are conscious living beings who have an equal right to be here. You are all dependent upon one another for survival. It is insane not to realize this now.

* Your children contain the original truth of your being that has been taught away. Many children now are fully equipped to assist in the creation of the next golden age on your planet. Nurture them; do not drug or abuse them; attempt to learn from them and

reawaken your original self, allowing direct access to us.

* Children know how to play and be joyful. These are important tools of creation. Allow the children to remind you how to play.

* Attempt not to blame, shame, or judge yourself, which facilitates doing these to others. You are all in the same process. You all chose to be here now to experience the most wonderful ascension process of your species and planet. Be compassionate, accepting, and forgiving to yourself and others, knowing you are all one. You are all here to love and support one another.

* Become aware of the perfection of nature and the cycle of creation on your planet. These cycles are the tools you need to learn (not control) to survive. You did not create the planet nor do you own it. You are here to better understand the perfection of your planet and learn how to care for it, thus one another.

* Together, we of the angelic realms with humanity can create a new world paradigm of We Consciousness/ Oneness. Call upon us regularly; we are here to love and support you.

HOW TO RECEIVE YOUR GOOD

Universal Law teaches,
You cannot receive
What has not been earned,
And those are the terms.

Many feel they deserve,
And wish to attain,
This and that.
But exactly what are the terms
Needed for the deserved to be served?

If you so resonate,
Emboss in your eternal memory bank
What is about to postulate.
So you can finally tank
What you think you rank in your bank, account.

Your earning is manifested knowing
There is but one Source and Force
For all good.
And that is the interior God-Presence,
Living in your inside residence.

This Shimmering Self
Is the Life Force flowing and growing
Through everyone and everything
That enables the entire Universe
To sing...

CHAPTER 8

COMPASSION FOR HOW YOU CHOSE TO LEARN

From Archangel Uriel, World Teacher and Guardian

Dear Beloved Humans,
If you could only feel the gratitude we of the higher realms have for the many challenging ways you have *chosen to learn what you came here to learn*, your hearts would burst. We applaud your often unknowing courage and determination to journey onward *to your divine soul plan destinations*. It has not been an easy pathway, but a necessary one to free you from all the constraints and restraints (you chose) that have polished and prepared you for your divine destiny *to become the master teachers of the universe.*

There was a time in your unrecorded past when things were united. There was a time when you loved in equality, harmony, and balance; you knew you were one with ALL THERE IS. For many reasons you chose for that to end; *to get as far from Oneness as possible in order to journey back to it.* **The journey has given you the tools and teachings you now need to**

know in order for you to be able to teach this to others (the purpose of all this).

Humanity is in process to return to a frequency of consciousness that will allow the planetary and human species soul plans to fully activate: to learn how to love in order to use this mighty tool as a building block of a new world paradigm of Oneness. You are students in these human bodies encompassed within the Lover-versity of life. **Your diploma is your multidimensional consciousness**, knowing you are eternal beings of light in human form for a brief moment, to learn what you need to learn, and free yourselves into divine bliss.

Once you can be in this 3-D dimension and higher ones at the same time, your journey becomes much easier. This allows you to have the wisdom to know and remember you are in process; remembering/ awakening that you live in a limitless universe that you are to experience and serve for eternity. No small mission, dear ones!

There have been many "bread crumb" teachings dropped along your pathway throughout time. Are you ready to pick up the crumbs and become who you are, and to fully embrace and embody why you came here? This teaching and others are here to assist you in remembering and finding what has been difficult for you to find. (See the many teachings within the Angel News Network that came directly from higher realms to further support you, www.theangelnewsnetwork.com.) **These will create transformational self-empowerment.**

In the past, there were dark forces that inserted corrupted belief systems into humanity. Many of you chose to adopt/accept these untrue beliefs into your lives and pass them on for generations. Many still exist today. This allowed others (the few controlling the many) to gain control and manipulate humanity. Remember, dear ones, it was part of your freedom of choice and will for this to take place, so you could learn the way you needed to learn. Perhaps there was no other way. **So accept with compassion and forgive how you needed to learn**. Keep your soul directed to where this is all leading—to the full activation of your soul plans in order to serve this world and others as master teachers. **You have experienced all aspects of creation: the good, the bad, the ugly, and the beautiful.**

You are moving through the healing of the governments, organized religions, and corporations that wished to limit your freedom and attempted to control you. **These are all based upon fear thinking**. Fear is an absence of love; *you are learning that you are love, and can give and receive love equally.* You ultimately cannot be controlled, nor can anything/anyone else, dear ones. **You are ready for these organizations that attempt to control you to now reflect the new paradigm of love of the people.**

The governments, religions, and corporations of the past—and, to some extent, still in the present—have reflected you, the people. *The Laws of Creation have reflected your emotions and thoughts,* and those of these organizations, in your weather patterns and natural events. This is the only way your planet can clear and cleanse herself of your abuse and perhaps shift your consciousness. Have you ever noticed how people come together after a large storm or natural disaster? A tough way to learn, but it is your choice, dear ones.

Can you now develop compassion and perhaps even gratitude for how you have chosen to learn, and begin to see the divine perfection in it all? By taking ownership of it all, you empower yourself and begin to remember.

SOURCE OF ALL

Love is the very Hub of Creation,
All love aspects are spokes
Off the hub creating a Wheel of Creation,
Manifesting loving elation.

Love is the Heart,
The force, the Source of all.
Can we now hear the call of our Hearts?
In scientific terms,
Love expresses itself
As the force between the source of electrons,
So everything can run.
Through love's force
The electron is Pure Spirit
Or God's Light,
Unconditional Love, Perfect,
All ways right.

The word is made flesh
Through the mesh of God's love.

Sweet thoughts or compassionate feelings,
Are activities of love reelings,
Within the human mind and heart.

Whoever makes themselves
Fully available and sits at the table
Of The Law of Love
Is completely able to always stay at that table.

Through our free thoughts and feelings
We have the power
Within every hour
To sink to our lowest thought or feeling,
Or rise to the highest.

CHAPTER 9

COSMIC CODES OF TRUTH

From the Council of Archangelic Realms (CAR)

Dear Beloved Earth Beings,
 Since there is very little truth in what you call reality, we would like to present **COSMIC CODES OF TRUTH**. Imagine your life and world redesigned around these cosmic truths, if you so choose. Master as many of these thirty codes as you can. Each one is your ticket to your divine destiny.

* Formless is ALL THERE IS.

* Unknowing is wisdom waiting.

* The portal to self-empowerment is your heart.

* You are One with the Light.

* You are transitioning from dense carbon to light crystalline.

* You are becoming formless in being the light.

* You are becoming One with the light.

* Light is your and your planet's final end.

* Know there are universal laws and equations you are mastering to be masters of them.

* Your knowing heart has stored within it, from all your lifetimes, all you need.

* You have agreed to everything you are experiencing; your **ownership** is your freedom.

* You are destined to become **universal master teachers** by mastering world service.

* You have had many lifetimes on this planet and others.

* Only by mastering **frequency and vibration** can you create your final golden age.

* You are all One: light, dark, right, wrong, male, female, problem, solution, duality, oneness, bad, good, fear, love, what is not, what is.

* All this is to learn to be and master love.

* Knowledge can become wisdom when applied when needed.

* Consciousness will allow your soul to become spirit.

* Only by experiencing all you have experienced can you release and free yourself of it.

* You have only begun to know and accept how amazing you are.

* You do not fully understand who and what your home planet is (a conscious living being).

* By knowing you are ONE with ALL THERE IS, you become it.

* Humanity is the key that opens the doorway to Oneness.

* You can only be free by knowing you are light born, not Earth born.

* You are the key to all wisdom, knowing there is only now.

* The Law that sent forth the light is the Word (Consciousness) of ALL THERE IS.

* The power of your word creates your life.

* The Word (Creation) came from chaos; calm the chaos and you have peace.

* Know that all is peace from chaos transmuted into light.

* Know that you are creation experiencing all aspects of itself to become the master teachers of the universe.

ALL ONE

In ALL space.
ALL things are One.
Though it seems divided,
Dualistic and separated,
It is only ONE.

ALL that exits,
Comes from the Light,
And that's ALL right.

ALL light comes,
Forth from the ALL,
Never being small.
ALL is,
ALL THERE IS

CHAPTER 10

CREATION EXPRESSED AND POWER OF THE WORD

From Archangel Uriel, World Teacher and Guardian

Greetings Beloved Children of Planet Earth,
   The Consciousness of Creation intended specific purposes for each of its creations. Let us **give** some examples for you to r**eceive** within your heart in order to manifest into your beingness and doingness:

Your planet created the beauty of **nature** to inspire (join to spirit/higher realms) humanity to rediscover and connect with your own divinity, and for you to also integrate with the frequency of your home planet. Your heart beats at the same megahertz of the planet.

Your body and Source created specific purposes for each part of itself. The purpose of your **emotional body** is to integrate dense form with the energy of life through your feelings (the most important aspect of being human). The purpose of your **mental body** is to inspire (to receive/connect with spirit/higher realms) perfection through your thoughts. The purpose of your **physical body**, through its consciousness, is to maintain and sustain the world of form.

Many of you know that your emotions and thoughts are creating your reality and lives all the time. That's how powerful and divine you are. And through taking ownership of that empowerment and divinity, you can discover how to manifest what it is you say you need—as long as it harms no other. This is what the ascended masters have achieved, dear ones.

One of the most powerful ways our emotions and thoughts become manifested is through the spoken word. **The spoken word is the pathway into the world of form**. This is the original purpose of the creation of language. Through the emotion and thought, and then the word, an action is formed. The key is to stay connected to your loving heart with the word and action.

Humanity has mastered duality and confrontation through the negative use of the words and actions. It is time, if you so choose, to realize all the pain and suffering caused by the misuse of the word and action, and know and take ownership of exactly what you have created. Then you can make another choice.

Dear children, as you move into your adulthood, it is time to commit to speaking words of equality, harmony, and balance (love). When you remember how to speak like an evolved being, you will be delighted how quickly the world around you transmutes into manifesting love, peace, and the abundance for which your weary world so hungers.

Remember, dear ones, what you create through your emotions, thoughts, and words comes back to you, whether it is love or separation. This is a universal law and a way the universe balances itself. Someday your man-made laws will be replaced with universal laws, as you become more conscious.

Right now, as best you can, make a commitment to speak, write, and act through love, compassion, and awareness. Be with others the way you wish them to be with you—no matter what. You can self-lovingly and powerfully express your truth, needs, and boundaries through your concern for how it affects others. As you have heard many times before, it is not what you say or write that creates duality and separation, and karma for yourself, it is the way you say it. Karma is an aspect of universal law that also supports the balance of all things. It would be a different world if more humans knew that karma actually existed and its effect on humanity. **Dear ones, become aware that all your emotions, thoughts, and words also affect and extend beyond this world.**

When you are not sure how to express yourself, take a deep breath and go into your knowing heart, **think with it**, and ask for guidance. You'll be amazed and delighted how compassionate and articulate you will become, and how you can transform a potentially challenging situation into a loving one. This is a demonstration of the **Law of Attraction** in this world and throughout the multiverse.

HOW TO CREATE

No form can come into creation
Without a thought as a picture.
For every thought contains an idea
That is the criteria of expression.

Let us look at the process
That brings access
To creation...

What is it you wish to create?
Is it worthy of your time and energy?
What is your reason to bring this into existence?
Is it to satisfy an addiction or comfort zone
Or get you arrested on the way home?

Make sure what you wish to create
Has no motive or need to do harm to another,
But has an intention of a loving brother.

Write down your plan in your own words,
As clearly and consciously as you can,
Then you have a starting plan...

Know you have the ability to create,
See it like a picture on a plate.

The seeing and the power to create
Are the gifts of God-state within?
Seeing and feeling within yourself
Allows you to lift creation off the shelf.

The heart already knows,
But keep reminding the mind
Creation is the ability
To see the God within all the time.
For God is the doer, the doing, and the deed,
And you through Him can create, and proceed with,
Whatever you need.

Read your written plan again and again
At the beginning and end of each day.
This way your creation is downloaded in your heart
That is the best part and start.
Keep your intention to yourself,
Hold its power inside you,
So only you know its view.

When you are ready,
Steady yourself and allow
You inner vision to come through,
Consciously connecting to the Law of Making
And the God within you to come fully come through...

Cast out all doubts and fear
And know in your heart
Your creation is near.

Have no set moment for results,
Just know you and God are issuing
The picturing of results,
With no wishing.

Allow yourself to be surprised and delighted,
And filled with gratitude
When your multitude, comes forth.

CHAPTER 11

DISCONNECT AND RECONNECT

From Archangel Uriel, World Teacher and Guardian, and Adama, Father of Humanity

Dear Beloved Earth Beings,

You have had six previous golden ages supported by higher realms that you initially trusted, then lost your trust and these ages fell. Once within a golden age, most often the mental body of mankind felt it could do it better its own way, no longer needing the support from sources outside the human mind. This pattern of behavior has repeated itself many times. You are once again at a crossroad of reconnecting with higher realms that are willing to support you into yet another golden age.

Dear ones, remember your lack of trust in something larger than you, outside yourself, has caused the fall of consciousness of mankind. The experiences you have had as a result of this have been very painful. This need to always be in control and to control others has created much imbalance in your lives and world. Look around your world now. What do you find?

When mankind decided they no longer needed the support of higher realms, and they could do it a better way on their own, **a misalignment was created between mankind and the higher realms. When you stopped following your own divinity, you separated from divinity itself.**

Today, many, many lifetimes later, there still exists a lack of trust in the forces that created and continue to support you. As a result of this, mankind has **created the monsters of fear, doubt, and ignorance**. Now you are being given another chance to tame these monsters, resume your trust, and find your way home again. Are you ready?

Your conscious living planet's soul plan has activated into creating a higher frequency of existence of equality, harmony, and balance. Thus, everything upon and within her body will be of the same frequency or will have moved elsewhere.

Your Mother Earth is no longer going to tolerate the abuses of humanity. We as a species are going to wake up or be walked out.

The new world paradigm is not going to be what your governments or corporations project or tell you. The reconnection with higher realms is in full force, thus your reconnection to your divinity. **The consciousness, or lack of, and the emotions and thoughts of mankind have created your present world** and governments, reflecting the people. Your weather systems and "natural events" are the result of the imbalances in mankind's being, and are the vehicle for the planet to clear and cleanse herself.

Mankind has not honored and has refused to understand the needs of the planet and their effect on humanity. Your behavior has been suicidal. **Dear ones, everything that has happened in your personal and global lives is the mirroring of the imbalances within yourselves**. The reflection of your fear, deceit, greed, and injustices are in full force. All the negative events are simply a mirror of what is out of balance on a human level.

The core issue is that mankind has not yet understood or taken ownership of how you are creating what you are creating. Dear ones, you create constantly, moment by moment, with your emotions and thoughts (expressed and unexpressed). You can think one thing and feel another, creating imbalance, and not supporting self, other, or the world.

It is time to become conscious of your emotions, thoughts, and actions. Words are the most powerful tool in the universe, and you support these words with the emotions powering them. But your words and emotions do not always support one another. Only through becoming conscious of this can it change. The universe is a fax machine; it will send back what it receives.

A reconnection to higher realms can allow a loving, gentle way to learn with grace and ease. Through our support, it does not have to be painful or difficult, the way you have chosen in the past and present, because you thought and felt you could do it a better way.

Your resistance to opening yourself to higher realms' support and easier ways is what creates the suffering in your lives.

Higher realms are not allowed to interfere in your lives and world unless you call upon us. Send us your trust and allow us to support and love you. Ask your mental body to return in service to your heart that knows all of which we speak. Learn to "think" with you heart, dear ones. Through the evolutionary path of your planet and species, you are being asked to be in service to your world and one another. Through your reconnection with us, you can choose to be in service to higher realms that allow your master teachership throughout the universe.

You have in your path a doorway to a new paradigm of oneness. Do you choose to walk through that doorway and close the door behind you? We are here to assist you in the creation of a final golden age on your planet. Are you ready to trust and allow us to assist you in moving fully into your divinity?

NO MATTER HOW

No matter how strange, or impossible
An experience seems, not possible
To our present state of being,
It is no proof, dear one,
That there isn't a greater roof
Of wisdom and law
Acting to produce no flaw
In greater wonder of creation
Around us in relation, all the time.

CHAPTER 12

DIVINE CREATIVE ENERGY EXPLAINED

From Archangel Uriel, World Teacher and Guardian, and Adama, Father of Humanity

Dear Beloved Children of Earth,

As an essential aspect of your awakening, and to better understand the unseen elements that maintain and sustain creation, let us discuss energy (since you are all condensed energy).

Energy is the smallest unseen element of life that creates everything, including you; your so-called elements of energy: atoms, electrons and neutrons, etc. (and you will soon realize there are even smaller measurements, as you further awaken). These elements of energy are intelligent, conscious, eternal forms gifted from Source/God/Creator.

These elements of energy respond to both mankind, through free will, and their original conscious creator, whose intention is love. Diversified forms of energy create your seen world. Even what was once called empty outer space you are now beginning to know is filled with the energy of creation: cosmic consciousness and divine love.

The elements of energy are determined by (divine or human) conscious thought; the frequency of energy is determined by emotions. As you are learning, consciousness, emotions, and thoughts are the factors of creation. Thus, the phrase "*love is the glue of creation*" is better understood, dear ones.

It is cosmic consciousness and divine love energy from Source that are the primary forces creating all things, since everything comes from the same "*Source-stuff.*" What you do with this energy is your choice through your freedom of will. Thus far in your recent history, you have not put it to very much good use.

To reiterate: initially, all energy is created from higher realms of cosmic consciousness and everlasting divine love. The initial energy is neutral and lovingly intended for the service of all life. Being in service, this energy becomes what your thoughts and emotions create. Again, now you better understand the power of your emotions and thoughts, dear ones.

Now, within your weary world, when you misuse energy that is intended for world service, with less than divine love and consciousness, you are creating duality, separation, and confrontation. This misuse of energy has a karmic consequence, which you are experiencing now in order to learn what you need to learn.

Dear ones, please know that you are given/gifted a lifetime of energy within each lifetime, an unlimited amount of energy for each incarnational cycle. You are free to create whatever you wish with the "supply from Source." Your lives are mirroring how you use the given energy right now. Are you having the life you say you want right now?

In truth, humanity has not yet mastered the right use of energy. The wisdom has been forgotten and is being remembered. By misusing energy for destructive purposes, mankind has created an unnecessary amount of pain and suffering. Are you ready to make a new choice?

All energy is intended to respond to love; when otherwise, this lack of responsibility has a consequence. The gift of energy was never intended for many of the destructive uses created by mankind. Where there is not love, there is destruction.

How do you think energy feels, being created from love, when you use it to kill one another, dear ones?

As mankind has misused energy for eons, it has become transmuted into the negative consciousness of your species and passed on through your DNA from one generation to another. Throughout your history you have seen the many consequences of this accumulated negative consciousness; past golden ages were destroyed by this misuse. Are you ready to make another choice in creating a final golden age on your planet?

Dear ones, you can create a world of equality, harmony, and balance with cosmic loving energy. Not all planets have free will, and your misuse of it and energy has been a powerful learning tool. What have you learned, dear ones? Would you like to make another choice now in the use of your free will and energy?

You can begin to use energy as a healing tool in all areas in your lives. Your thoughts and emotions can create other uses of energy in freeing yourselves from yourselves. Soon you can know that there is enough free energy to power your entire planet and re-create your governmental and economic structures.

The path to this new use of energy is your self-mastery, learning how to fully love yourself and others. Dear ones, the divine light use of energy will eliminate old age, disease, lack, and limitation, and create blissful immortality.

Learning does not have to be so difficult; it is your ignoring/applying your lessons/learning that makes it so. Aren't you tired of learning through "what is not"? Soon the time will arise when you no longer misuse your free will and energy, and take responsibility for being divine.

Dear ones, there is no escaping the cosmic consequences of the misuse of your free will and gifted energy. Why not make the shift with your planet to love and be in WE CONSCIOUSNESS now! All your higher selves are good. Why not awake and fully express that divine aspect of self now!

CREATION OF PLANET EARTH

The entire cosmic universe
Was involved and ignited
In the creation of planet Earth.

Twelve Star systems came together
To bring the best of each star
Into our reach from afar.

It was called the grand divine experiment
Inspired by unconditional love,
So they called us,
The Lover-versity of Love.

The whole universe is waiting
And watching us now
To see if we can ace this
Final place, the final Golden Age.

To learn to love self and another is the mission
In order to become the master teachers
And preachers of love,
And be the love stuff of submission.

In recent years we have discovered
Billions of galaxies,
Many like us.
Needing to learn like us
About the reality of love.

Are we ready to accept
That this immense galactic universe
Is not averse to a total
Connection through affection.

CHAPTER 13

DO YOU SEE ME AS THEE?

By Phillip Elton Collins

Do you see me as thee?
The real reason I exist, for thee,
Is for you to see me, as thee.

For in fact, we are **ONE**,
In order for me to be thee.

If we can only really see,
That you and me create
The WE to be truly free.

Once free, we can see
That we simply be,
In order to serve the WE...

All this *WE-BEING*
Is created through you,
Loving you enough,
To see as me,
For WE is the real reason
To be.

LOVE: LAW OF LIFE

We know the old adage,
Love Is All There Is.
Well, the ole Masters say it
This way: There is only One Law of Life,
And that is Love.

Love is the highest vibration in Creation,
Allowing all manifestation making.

Through man's thoughts, emotions and deeds
Man really never ceases
Creating his needs.

The absence of love
Is ever present,
Most often in fear, ever near.

That not of love
In effect becomes self-centered darkness
Moving in its own orbit,
Not allowing any love sparkness.

When the Law of Love is enforced
All negativity goes to sleep,
And we have no need to weep.

Through love the glorious God-Power
Within you awakens,
You release and express love
And there are no longer any hateful hours.
For you have allowed
The love-flowers, to bloom,
And there will be no further room
For anything other than what love can swing and bring...
Love is the vibration and glue
That created everything,
Especially YOU.

CHAPTER 14

EAST/WEST STRUGGLE

*Current Events Bulletin from the Council
of Archangelic Realms (CAR)*

B eloved Children of Earth,
   What you continue to see in your world's current events
is your continued fight for separation, reflecting your wounds
and ego defenses. Who is right, who is wrong, and who is in
control?

**Dear ones, there is neither right nor wrong nor
control!** When are you going to learn and know this wisdom
that lives within your KNOWING hearts? Your present East/
West divide is *"a fight to be right,"* concealing much deceit and
denial of that deceit. Governments reflect the people they are
governing. Do you wish to make some new choices that reflect
your higher selves?

*Hidden behind your governmental blusters are the real reasons
to control the planet's natural resources*; resources that only your
Mother Earth truly possesses, that support her life stream,
thus, the well-being of all life upon and within her body. We
of the archangelic and other realms cannot interfere with your

freedom of will/choice, nor do we have any desire to do so. But we do desire to assist your awakening and destiny to evolve into a higher state of being.

The irony and blessing within your current "world drama" is that most of your developed world is now economically tied together; **what affects one, affects all**. This just may be your saving grace, dear ones. Your real threat to one another is the wounded and ego defense behavior of those you choose or allow to be in power, dear ones. If you choose, it is time to **stop giving your power away** to those who do not support the highest good of all the people.

If you choose, dear humanity, it is time to take your power back. We have **gifted you with cyberspace** communication systems that allow you to free yourself from those who attempt to control you. Can you release yourselves from the abuses and addictions associated with these communication systems and use them as intended? Within higher realms none are allowed to lead or sit in council unless they have achieved true spiritual growth.

Your transportation (it is your destiny to teleport) and communication systems (soon you will resume your telepathy) can link you all together in **communities of equality, harmony, and balance**. Can you begin to see you cannot survive without one another; that you are truly one? You don't have to kill one another to arrive at this truth! Can you see the folly in all the "sword waving," and that the emperor truly has no clothes? **Your self-empowerment is the clothes, dear ones.**

YOU are the loving self-empowerment, not others. You are discovering the divine power within yourselves, a process of inside out, not outside in. Since your governments reflect the people they govern, why not **send a new reflection out into the world**—one of We Consciousness and truth—remember, "WE THE PEOPLE, FOR THE PEOPLE."

If you so choose, stand up, Beloved Children of Earth, and let yourself and your leaders know that their wounds, ego defenses, and hidden agendas (at your expense) are no longer within your soul plan!

WHEN MANKIND BECOMES...

There is so much waiting
From higher realms to be given,
To humanity when we are ready,
And steady enough to receive it.

These new truths and wisdoms
Will change our lives for the better
Whether we know it now or not.
When we have the credentials,
The essentials will be revealed.

When mankind stops generating,
And creating destruction throughout
The land, we shall land in a new paradigm,
That will swell into heaven.

Through our disastrous feelings and thoughts,
Spread to the seen and unseen worlds,
Our intense vibrations are placed in many places and spaces.
They hook themselves to humanity,
And we create insanity, again and again.

Humanity seems to have no understanding
Of what happens when we send
Our hateful stuff out into the rough.
Of life.

The feeling aspect of us is feminine,
From the activity of our heart space.
The thought side is masculine,
From the activity of our mental body.

Let us now allow the male and female to balance,
As the mind returns into service to heart,
So we never have to part again.

CHAPTER 15

ELEMENTS OF ETERNAL YOUTH AND IMMORTALITY

Inspired by Archangels Chamuel and Charity

Dear Beloved Humans,
You are eternal spiritual beings having a human experience. You've all heard this phrase. You somewhat understand the concept of immortality as part of your spiritual components, but what elements are necessary for you to actually manifest your *divine destiny* to be eternally youthful and immortal?

SEVEN SACRED TENETS OF ETERNAL YOUTH AND IMMORTALITY

ONE: Within every present moment, intend and reiterate your intention to be youthful and immortal. The Universe is a fax machine and will deliver exactly what the impeccability, or not, of your emotions, thoughts, words, or actions send to it.

TWO: *Maintain and sustain absolute constancy in your intentions and willingness to be and do what the higher realms are teaching you about how to manifest what it is you say you want. The path to your destination lies within you, not outside yourself. It is waiting to be awakened by your awareness (consciousness). The solution has never been a secret, it has always been inside you, but you have ignored opening the door. For eons you have looked outside yourself for an external source to tell you what to do.* **The solution is your true spiritual transformation.**

THREE: *Accepting with compassion, thus forgiving and knowing that the external sources (Mom, Dad, religion, government, etc.) are not the solution. The solution is your relationship with you; creating a self-loving relationship will empower you to your destination.*

FOUR: *Your DNA is the next essential element. Your DNA evolves at the speed that you evolve in your consciousness and increases your love of self and others. Your body is a reflection (mirror) of consciousness. As it evolves, your emotional, mental, and physical bodies will begin to mirror the raised consciousness you have achieved.* **Evolving into your eternal youth and immortality has always been inside you; your raised consciousness has to activate it.**

FIVE: *Your emotions, thoughts, words, and actions are the fifth element. Do you see yourself as good enough and worthy enough to achieve what you desire? What is the quality of your internal dialogue or dialogue with others? Does it always reflect what it is you say you want to achieve? Remember, you are eternal beings, with only the limits you are taught or place upon yourself. Do not allow anyone or anything to limit you!*

SIX: *Your eternal youth and immortality are a* **state of being***. To activate this truth, you must unite with it and become it. Eternal youth and immortality are a 5-D tool of pure light (who you truly are). In order to activate this light, you need to increase the light within all the cells of your physical and etheric bodies. You then need to clear and cleanse (which many of you are in the process of now during this ascension opportunity) your emotional body of all negative emotions, monitor your thoughts, and think like an ascended master (where you are headed). Allow your believing mind to fully go back in service to the* **knowing heart that knows exactly how to be and do all this!** *Begin to know and see what an amazing vessel your physical body is. It is up to all individuals to change their perception regarding their bodies and learn how to utilize their full potential that they are innately endowed with.*

SEVEN: *Begin to live the new life you have found and no longer need to seek.* **Eternal youth and immortality are located in your very own mind and heart***. You will be surprised and delighted when you realize how simple it is to be who you truly are.*

ETERNAL YOUTH?

Is there such a thing as eternal youth?
Is it really real?
If so, how do we appeal,
To reveal it?

Let us see if we can unmask,
And move away the trash
In order to mix the recipe
To maintain and sustain
What remains, forever?

One Mighty Ascended Master
Has called eternal youth,
God's gift to Himself to His creation.

He goes on to explain,
Eternal youth is the flame of God
Abiding in the body of man,
Making him over, forever, more.

As we look closer at this youthful recipe
We see,
Eternal perfection can only be rightly achieved
By permanently casting out
All dense, negative light, in order to get it right.

There must be peace, love and light
Expressed in the outer self
For eternal youth and beauty
To be expressed as a Supreme Duty.

Youth, beauty and perfection
Are the attributes of
Love, which the God-Self

Is continually sustaining
And maintaining in its creation.

Through your emotions and thoughts
You can create vibrations
That shift your relations
Of self and others
Into a youthful formula,
Forming immortality.

For only feeling separate from self and Source,
Can you prevent eternal youth and beauty,
Coming forth...

CHAPTER 16

FIVE PRIMARY
EGO DEFENSES

From Archangel Gabriel, adapted by Phillip Elton Collins

When the founders of the Angel News Network were being trained as light ascension therapists through the teachings of Archangel Gabriel, the FIVE PRIMARY EGO DEFENSES were an essential teaching. As healing arts therapists, this important teaching gives insights into the cause and effect of many emotional, mental, or physical imbalances. It explains the **how and why of so much of life**. This wisdom can and will be a game-changer in our world, and a powerful tool in the activation of your soul plan.

At this crucial time within our planetary and personal evolution into higher consciousness, all past and present lives' "woundings" are rising up in order to be released, cleared, cleansed, and healed. Wounds from past and present lifetimes often have a great deal of emotions associated with them. In order to heal the wounds and release them, it is necessary to know and feel the emotions inside them. To think we are our wounds has created much of the lack, limitation, and duality/confrontation in our world.

Wounded and defensive little boys and girls with a lot of power are controlling our world. Let us imagine and create a world where our leaders have a self-loving, empowered relationship with self, thus others.

A **defense** is an unconscious reaction to protect the wound. In effect, the protective defense is an etheric "armoring" around the wound. Until the unconscious becomes conscious, lifetimes of patterns and comfort zones will continue. As quantum physics has proven, the moment the wound and defense are fully seen, they will shift and begin to dissolve into the illusion they are; for we are not our wounds and defenses, but they have controlled us for eons.

In order to break the insane cycle of wounds and defenses, let us now become conscious of them. We each have a primary (monadic) defense leading our lives, but in reality we have aspects of each defense within us. See if you can identify your primary defense. Knowing who we are is essential in freeing ourselves from ourselves. The names of these defenses do not reflect standard psychotherapy definitions, but they expand into metaphysical energetic healing.

ORAL DEFENSE

The oral defense forms earliest, since the first thing we do is suckle. It defines itself through one who can never be enough, thus the person seldom can be fulfilled. The person has a "vampire" energy, pulling and sucking energy from others. These people appear always busy, never having enough time.

The **primary emotion** is feeling **weak—low self-worth, not good enough.** The **parental upbringing** is often deprivation, not being nurtured, taking care of parents' needs. The **past life** issues center on starvation and deprivation. Therefore, this defense is trying to be filled by pulling energy from others, with no boundaries. Their **basic need** is to integrate fulfilling the self and setting boundaries. The **body type** is caved in or hunched over slightly, with vacant eyes.

MASOCHIST DEFENSE

The masochist defense reflects a fear of being controlled (by Mom or Dad) or subjugated by others, and thus the need to flee inside. The essence of the individual is held inside or distorted. These people appear quiet and fearful of being taken over by others. They have a tendency to sink energy within themselves and have difficulty resonating with a distinct moment in time, getting lost.

The **primary emotion** is humiliation, feeling deprived or lost. The **parental upbringing** is an overbearing mother consumed with her needs. The **past life** issues are about being imprisoned or trapped. Therefore, people in this defense will withdraw, and depend on others to tell them what they need or when to act. Their **basic need** is an ability to express/feel/achieve individuality and boundaries. The **body type** is solid, padded, often overweight.

PSYCHOTIC DEFENSE

The psychotic defense is a reaction to the feeling of betrayal, with overt aggressive behavior toward others. They need to have an enemy in order to feel superior. A warrior energy is projected through the cause of right and wrong. The basic energy is a pulling and pushing out over the head. There is a tendency to project time into the future, not the now.

The **primary emotion** is not trusting in order to avoid betrayal. There is a fear of being out of control or unsafe. The **parental upbringing** is based upon one parent against the other and feeling used by the mother. The **past life** is all about betrayal. Therefore, there is little trust at present. The **basic need** is to be able to trust the self, make mistakes, and see others as equal. The **body type** is a developed upper body and large back.

SCHIZOID DEFENSE

The schizoid defense is based upon the fear to exist in the physical. There are many past and present life traumas projected into what is perceived to be a threatening world. Therefore, escaping the body is a way out of the pain, since it is felt that the body is not a safe place to be. This defense is often seen as multidimensional or having multiple personalities. Many channels and psychics of other frequencies contain aspects of this defense.

The **primary emotion** is feeling unsafe, a fear of abandonment and separation. The **parental upbringing** is one of abuse and attack. The **past life** issues include torture or punishments for beliefs. Thus, they cannot integrate God-self into the physical, with no boundaries. The **basic need** is integrating being human into spirituality. The **body type** is slight and weak.

RIGID DEFENSE

This is one of the last defenses to develop, usually during our early teenage years. This defense is associated with the need to appear perfect in an imperfect world. The individual develops a division between true inner feelings and the outer world. To appear perfect and project that image is vital. Not able to see (blind spot) anything negative with self, pushing and deflecting their energy forward while avoiding true intimacy. Life is filled with an endless succession of empty moments. The **primary emotion** is emptiness and a fear of making mistakes.

The **parental upbringing** is relationships with no real connection of feelings. The **past life** issue is who is in charge with what image; loss of sense of individuality; not in reality, appropriate response for image. The **basic need** is to realize that the sense of self is on the inside; get off the treadmill to be real. The **body type** is to look perfect.

IN CONCLUSION

By using these defense tools within a therapeutic personal process, we can free ourselves from ourselves and create a world of equality, harmony, and balance, reflecting the loving relationship with self and our divine soul plan.

PAST LIVES

If we could only remember,
And understand that
Repeated Earth lives
Are an optimistic opportunity
To take ownership, correct and balance

Mistakes of past lives,
Becoming a true member of life.

Then we just might
Use every experience
To make a legal contract with learning,
Instead of resisting,
All we create,
Not seeing ourselves as victims,
Always persisting.

When we finally become conscious,
Of the purpose of past lives,
Learning the lessons of each one,
Then we can leave the
Rotating wheel of incarnations,
Through free will,
And become immortal, at last.

CHAPTER 17

HEADS-UP ON
WORLD EVENTS

From the Intergalactic Federation
Current Events Bulletin (CEB)

*D*ear Beloved Sisters and Brothers on Planet Earth,
  This is another Current Events Bulletin from higher realms
supporting your freedom of choice and will, and your highest good:

  Once again there are hidden forces on your planet attempting to
enter you into conflict with one another for their profit and gain. This
is an age-old tactic that the powerful few have used for eons to control
you. The presented "facts" are never the real reason things are unfolding as they are. Use your resonance and discernment to know the truth,
remain in neutrality, and maintain and sustain a unity consciousness,
if you so choose.

  You have been gifted with Ethernet (cyberspace) technologies to
allow you to gain more of the truth, bypassing controlled forms of communication and sharing it with one another. We of the Intergalactic
Federation are observing events as they unfold and wish to give you a
heads-up at this time. We are multigalactic guardians of your planet,

solar system, and galaxy. We nor no one else can interfere with your freedom of choice and will. How do you now choose to learn?

Again, use your resonance and discernment (your internal gyro system) to determine what is true for you. As a last play for power and control at this time, there are many hidden forces on your planet attempting to distract and separate you from one another.

Your hearts are an internal system of knowing what is true and supports your highest good. What do you choose?

WITHIN EACH OF US

Within each of us
Is the same power that can
Be expressed by higher beings
In any hour.

If you merely choose
To use this power of the hour.

Each human has a freedom of choice
To express their higher self,
Or something else.

You are the chooser
Of your own expression,
The Self-Conscious Creator
That no longer has to be the loser.

At any time you can choose
To rise above lack and limitation,
And any imitation of life.

Simply apply all your energy and determination
And you will achieve all your needs,
And succeed.

Now know, Dear Ones,
The God in you
Is always directing,
And perfecting
The Master inside you.
What do you choose?

CHAPTER 18

HELPFUL HINTS ON HEALING

From Archangel Raphael

Dear Beloved Humans in need of healing, We Energies of Healing greet you,

All your health issues, whether physical or mental or whatever your accepted medical community calls them, are created by imbalances within your emotional body. In order to balance and heal the physical or mental bodies, you must first recognize and release the feelings (emotions expressed) that cause the imbalance. When balance is restored in the emotional body, the rest of you will entrain to the emotional balance, and true healing can become everlasting.

Emotions are one of the most important aspects of humanity and the least understood. *Emotions are the (energetic) dynamic expression of your divinity within this frequency.* Many of you often cannot access your emotions due to your conditioning and belief systems. Many have been taught that good boys and girls simply do not express how they feel. Thus, many emotions become suppressed.

Through the misuse of your freedom of choice and will, unexpressed and uncontrolled negative emotions have created great stress within your physical and mental bodies and throughout your world. These unexpressed emotions not only collect within your atmosphere, creating your weather and affecting world events, they collect in your bodies, creating havoc and dis-ease.

It is time to become conscious of your emotions, their cause, and their effect on you and your world. Many of your emotions are your wounded little boy or girl screaming through his/her wounds and ego defenses to be heard. From higher realms, there are many teachings on wounds and defenses available to you. It is time to absorb these truths and stop seeking other solutions.

It is time to wake up and know how to heal by knowing the cause and effect.

All true healing requires an investment in and deep examination of the self. It is time to apply the wisdom and teachings presented to you here again. As you heal your inner pain and trauma, you will heal not only your physical and mental bodies but also all the difficult situations in your life.

External pain and difficulties mirror your inner pain and fears. *These reflect what needs to be transmuted through your consciousness.* When your emotional body is not in perfect balance, it affects all other aspects of your being.

By transforming your consciousness through the balancing of your emotional body, you are integrating higher vibrations that will transform all of you (and your world).

Dear ones, you actually have emotions embedded in your emotional body from past and present lives. These were the result of lessons you chose to learn during your ascension process. Now is the time for the final cleansing, clearing, and healing of all this.

You all have emotional trauma and pain from your many lifetimes stored within your DNA that has been passed along from lifetime to lifetime. Are you ready to finally release all this, which is no longer serving you? We are here to assist you at this time of opportunity by teachings such as this; **to assist your complete and true healing by assisting in the removing of your many layers of emotions to reveal the true you: a divine being without any imbalance or limitation.**

Call upon us as you sleep to further assist your specific healing. During your sleep you will absorb new truths about yourself and factor them into your waking consciousness. Dear ones, **your awakened state to your divinity is your eternal medicine.**

As a complete healing takes place, the emotional cause is released (the most important aspect of your healing). If you so choose, it is time to release all feelings of rage, anger, sadness, abandonment, betrayal—pain and suffering in your soul and the soul of humanity that you have carried far too long.

The time has come to thoroughly heal the past and the present, and embody and embrace a new you and world paradigm of equality, harmony, and balance. Dear ones, **your heart is the direct link to your soul and Source;** it holds all of you always. Through opening and trusting your heart and loving yourself, you can release and heal all old and present negative emotions.

For many, negative emotions have become comfort zones, habits, patterns, and old friends to hold near no matter what. But it is time to release all that no longer serves your highest good nor is a good use of your energy. Your emotions have consumed a large portion of you. Where you are headed, they will not exist nor be needed.

The healing process is a unique personal process for each of you, since you are all unique. Endeavors such as the Angel News Network offer much support in this process. Are you ready to submit to whatever process is necessary to free yourself from yourself? **You are being offered one of the greatest ascension opportunities ever. Are you ready to join us and be free at last?**

AREN'T WE TIRED OF GROWING OLD YET?

We know the cells in our body
Are not so oddly programmed for eternal life.
So why don't we honor our cell design,
And live all the time.

Higher realms are quite puzzled
Why humanity continues its struggle
Of self-created lack and limitation
Where we insist upon decay and disintegration.

It is quite puzzling how humanity
Is blind as to why our bodies and mind
Seem to continue to fold and grow old.
So if our cells can eternally renew
Why can't you?
Why do we as a race,
Seem content to continue death,
At such a good pace?

While we clasp to youth,
And beauty and life,
We still hold onto our strife.
So what we cling to most,
Can't be boasted in life.

Just maybe it all has to do
With our losing our connection
To our Inner-Power-Presence,
While looking outside self,
For all the inside message.

And let us also balance and check
Our immobilizing emotions and terrorizing thoughts,
At the door, that's a good idea too,
Then we'll never have to grow old, anymore.

CHAPTER 19

PATHWAYS TO ASCENSION

From Archangel Gabriel

Dear Beloved Children of Ascension,

It is your divine destiny to evolve beyond the vibrational existence in which you find yourself at this time. It is your soul plan to join the higher-realm frequencies from whence you came, and who maintain and sustain you at present, creating a new world paradigm of equality, harmony, and balance. Please know within your hearts, dear ones, we of the higher realms have a great deal of gratitude for the choices you have made to support the evolution of your planet, solar system, and galaxy to become the master teachers of other worlds. We know it has not always been an easy path in the past and present, but we wish to assure you that no matter how your present may appear, there is a divine destiny of higher-realm existence awaiting you. It's just a matter of how and when for each of you.

Let us discuss some *pathways* **that will assist in the journey you have chosen being human.**

Pathway # 1

Please know that all you are currently experiencing is a not-so-simple clearing and cleansing, thus a healing of your emotional, mental, and physical bodies that have created your present reality. No density can be permitted into the higher realms. This process will allow the reinstatement of your eternal higher selves and your I Am Presence.

Pathway # 2

You are presently in 3-D existence, and you experience the 4-D when you sleep and during so-called death. Each dimension has a certain frequency, which you are beginning to create within yourselves. The 5-D where you are headed is achieved when your consciousness maintains and sustains that same frequency all the time. Then you permanently entrain to that higher frequency through your resonance. Once there, you become immortal.

Pathway #3

The organ of ascension is your knowing heart. Your ascended being has always lived within your heart. You are simply learning how to awaken and access it. Until you have ascended fully, simply act like an ascended being, retraining your emotional and mental bodies. Your ascended being is actually present all the time, dear ones.

Pathway #4

The duality, separation, and confrontation that your wounds and ego defenses have created must vanish. Stop believing in right and wrong and control in your 3-D world. They are all aspects of the same thing. Begin to access what's in your loving, knowing heart, not what's in your mental body, and begin being and living that frequency daily. Become ready to reprogram your nervous system that has become addicted to duality, separation, and confrontation. You are not separate. You are oneness and love, dear ones. You have brought yourselves to near destruction and learned all you need to learn from "what is not." Are you ready to make some new choices? We await you knowing and being this!

Pathway #5

Through Pathways #4, you have learned quite well how to shame, blame, and judge yourself, which projects to others. What you see in another is simply an unhealed aspect of you, dear ones. Can you accept with compassion, thus forgive this lack of self-love, and begin to know yourself as a divine being? The foundation to your divinity and a new world is you loving you.

Pathway #6

Your spiritual DNA awakening and higher chakras (eight through twelve) activation at this time are the tools you need to allow your direct connection to the higher frequencies where you are permanently headed. Until you fully arrive, we are here to love and support your journey.

Pathway # 7

One of the grandest reunions taking place is you and your I AM PRESENCE, which can connect you to your individuated divine soul plan. Your I AM PRESENCE is an innate gift, a force from creation that allows you to know/remember who you are and why you are here. Your life, your beingness, exists eternally within the timeless frequency of your I AM PRESENCE.

Pathway #8

There are many myths and untruths as to exactly what ascension is and when it will take place. What you will be able to do when you ascend is not the primary purpose of ascension. What is important is what the value and purpose of ascension will mean for you as an individual. Each of you is unique and has a unique path (soul plan) to your higher self/frequency. This is yours to discover, your journey.

Pathway # 9

Everything upon and within your planet is composed of the same energy (atoms/electrons). Thus, you are all from the same *sacred stuff. This includes the seen and the unseen around you. The unseen forces, the conscious minerals, the breathing plants, the stewards of the planet, the animals and the human species,* all are interrelated and needed to make life possible. One is not better than another, nor is it to be controlled by the other. An essential component of higher-frequency existence is the consciousness of harmlessness by knowing the sacredness of all life cohabiting your precious planet. Karma will balance all harm.

Pathway # 10

An essential part of the clearing and cleansing mentioned earlier is retraining your nervous systems from the old comfort zones and negative patterns/habits that have brought you to near destruction. The Angel News Network and many other endeavors offer many pathways to achieving this. (See the Life Mastery program, www.theangelnewsnetwork.com.) The key to releasing the old programming is your self-love.

Pathway # 11

Major tools for your ascension are your own resonance and discernment (your internal gyro systems), and the emotions of joy and bliss that will empower your process with grace and ease. If it seems like work, it will be work. Again, it is your divine destiny to ascend into higher frequencies of existence. Demand and command the universe through your resonance, discernment, and grace to ease the pathway.

Pathway # 12

Love is the highest frequency within the universe. It is the building block of everything. All is maintained and sustained by love. Without love there is no creation, only destruction. Love will always bring our emotions and thoughts into oneness. The organ of love is your heart. Your heart knows that love is all there is; everything else is the absence of love. We are all here to learn to love. A key equation in the universe is GRATITUDE = ABUNDANCE. When you learn to have gratitude for all that is in your life (not absent), it will create (more) abundance. The combination of love and an attitude of gratitude will greatly facilitate your ascension process.

Pathway # 13

Your intention to ascend to higher frequencies needs to become the major focus of your life. You must be willing to have a harsh examination of self and be willing to release all unhealed aspects of self. Ascension always begins with each one of you in a process of inside out, not outside in. If you are willing to be these things, you are on an authentic pathway to ascension and soul plan activation.

MASTERY MATTERS

What does it take to achieve Self-Mastery?
To have conscious control
Of all forces
And be able to manipulate all matter
The adept student blabbers.
The Master replies:
First, you must know your own God-Self, in the WE,
Second, have neutral feelings in all relations and creations,
And third, be not able to misuse gained power, through the ME.

For you are a star bound to a body,
And when you free WE from the ME
The star within you
Will shine bright for eternity!

CHAPTER 20

HONOR THE BODY TEMPLE

From Archangel Uriel, World Teacher and Guardian

Dear Humans housed in a physical body,
There is an eternal cosmic relationship between your physical body, your planet, and the cosmos. All are made of the same elements and are dependent upon one another. What affects one, affects all.

At present, there are certain cultural factors within some of your behavior in relationship with your bodies that reflect an acute imbalanced relationship with self, others, the planet, and the cosmos.

Dear ones, your bodies are not billboards to be written upon, pierced, branded, or distorted in any way. This current behavior reflects an imbalanced relationship with self—a mirroring out that has reached critical mass. Through your freedom of choice and will, we ask, "Would you like to become conscious of your behavior and begin to make another choice, or learn what you need to learn by continuing your behavior and its consequences?"

The procedures, inks, and toxins that you are introducing into your physical bodies can create consequences you call disease and distortion. **The need to treat your body this way is a reflection of your wounds, a lack of nurturing by self and othe**rs. By adding extra elements to an already perfect form, you are saying, "Can you love and accept me now? I am not 'good enough' the way I originated."

*Dear ones, what within you can you not accept that the forces that created you already knew to make a perfect reflection of themselves? **Perhaps it is time to reconnect with those forces**. You are perfect just the way your body was born; do you need to permanently adorn?*

If you so choose, place live, organic foods and pure water in your body proper that houses your eternal being. Honor your body in all ways. You need not alter it in any way. YOU ARE THE SACRED STEWARDS OF PERFECT CREATION.

The electronics that higher realms have gifted to humanity are meant to free you from 3-D controls. They are not meant to become addictions or to create further separation. Your bodies are not designed to have a constant vibration and frequency of these electronics. Constantly assaulting your senses/nervous system will create imbalances within your body. If you so choose, use your discernment as to how these gifts are used, and become aware of the ironic separation that is being created by these gifts that are meant to free you.

Dear ones, what is it within your relationship with self that prevents you from being silent and quiet, connecting with your higher self? **This direct connection will reveal your soul plan and your purpose in being here**. Your nervous system does not need to be constantly stimulated to know you are alive or good enough to be alive.

Beloved humans, you are perfect just the way you are. Pause a moment before you feel a need to alter your physical body or misuse use it in any way. Connect with your heart and ask, "What portion of me needs healing to accept me with compassion just way I am?" You might just be surprised and delighted with the answers that come.

Dear ones, no tattoo, piercing, branding, or electronic adornment will make you any more acceptable and perfect than you already are! What do you choose? It will forever be your choice. When you choose the choices that serve your highest good, those choices serve your planet and the cosmos equally.

A RAGE WITHIN

What mysterious opiate origin lies deep within humanity's ancestral rage?

From whence came its ancient source that can kill and conquer, we ask?

It lives deep within us all. And yet it can frighten us when it reveals its cruel countenance in duality and confrontation.

What is the cause, knowing its effect, of this monstrous force, we ask?

The moment is upon us to understand, release, and heal this ugly anger from our being that has kept us imprisoned so long.

Dear Souls, this ragged rage comes from our so many golden ages, loss. Loss due to our "mighty minds" that thought they could control creation, replace it, be it.

A fierce force came upon us that could not, would not accept and trust our divinity, and connection to creation, when once we could.

As humanity went its own way, deep within we knew we had lost something most precious. We became enraged at self for being so selfish, so foolish.

This self-rage has reflected out and created much of the madness in our world for a millennium.

Throughout the eons we have carried this self-sabotaging sense, and inflicted it upon self, each other, and our unconditionally loving home, Mother Earth.

Dear Souls, the time has come to accept with compassion, thus forgive how we have chosen to learn, through our freedom of will and choice.

It is time to reconnect with Creation. To know we are a divine aspect of it.

We have traveled as far from the truth as possible. Let us now turn around and head home.

When now, at last again we consciously connect with creation, our rage shall ramble away like an angry child replaced by cosmic love, as adults.

For only through our connection to creation can we embrace our final golden age in service to ALL THERE IS.

Are we ready to release our furious face and create a world knowing we are God experiencing self? An equal, balanced world without the angry "me," replaced by the loving "we."

CHAPTER 21

HOW SELF, LIFE, AND DEATH RELATE

From Archangel Uriel, World Teacher and Guardian

Dearly Beloved Humans,

You are individuated expressions of Creation expressing itself. Your life and the thing you call death are but reflections and pathways to the relationship with self. Now you are beginning to understand the expression "the only relationship you are having is the one with self," and how this relates to creation itself.

Human life in dense 3-D human formatting is but a brief presence (moment) within the eternity of your immortal existence. Dear ones, you have all had thousands of lifetimes on this planet, to learn what you needed and agreed to learn to become the master teachers of the universe by first starting to learn to be in **world service** to this planet and one another. All your lifetimes have been a short duration with your total relationships from whence you came (Source/God).

It's difficult for many of you to know that it is essential that you **have joy and bliss** while you are in this frequency of Earth's "Lover-versity" and learning; the only reason you enrolled in being here. These vibrations of joy and bliss can power (empower) you through the entire process of human life, or not. In fact, each and every one of you is an essential component of life or you simply would not be here. **Your individuated human cycles of life are what are powering the entire evolution of the planet and human species; some call this ascension.**

Together, all of you—through your emotions, thoughts, and actions—are the "*manifestation machine*" of the Earth herself. Your emotions, thoughts, and actions are creating the very weather itself, affecting the seasons and many of the "natural" acts-of-God events. You know how your man-made governments, religions, and corporations (that mirror your psyche) have affected everything. Now you are beginning to **remember how powerful you are**.

Once you can take **ownership** of all this, it can become a game-changer in your lives and world. You just might begin to make other choices through your freedom of choice and will.

Sacred geometrics, synchronicity, and Universal Laws of Creation and Love become the **spokes of a cosmic wheel that cycles the planet and all** (minerals, plants, animals, 5-D civilizations) upon and inside the planet. *In effect, a vehicle (merkaba) is created by the relationships of humanity, the planet, and the cosmos that creates the "ride" you call life*. This creates all you need to nourish you and allows your divine destinies to meet their destination, as long as you are within this human frequency evolving to higher ones.

Let us focus on the **cosmic creative elements of Love**, not the human emotion or what you may think love is. *Love is the energetic building block and glue that is holding everything together.* Without your loving vibration support of self, one another, and the planet, creation has a rough time of it. How you have abused yourselves and the planet is a good case in point. **Your lack of compassion and your ignorance have brought you to near destruction.** This behavior is hampering all which we have spoken of earlier within this teaching. It is time to wake up and take responsibility for *being the stewards of self, one another, and the planet* or there will be a consequence not to your liking. In fact, you won't be allowed to stay here as a karmic consequence.

As many of you know, the planet's soul plan has been activated to ascend into a higher frequency of existence; thus, all upon and inside the planet will become the same frequency or be transported elsewhere. Sounds a little harsh, but no harsher than this patient planet has been treated. It's called survival. And the universe knows exactly how to do that. **Humanity did not create the Earth nor do you own it**, in spite of your man-made laws and governments.

You have killed millions of yourselves fighting over something you never owned. How insane is that?!

If you so choose, it is time to move from thinking you own something to knowing you are the loving stewards of a precious divine experiment in diversity and learning how to love.

Your attempting to conquer the world has not worked out very well. Why not attempt to love and nurture it now? The reward is the survival of your planet and yourselves. Consider creating *attitudes of gratitude* that allow the creation of communities of equality, harmony, and balance that include you and the planet. Focus on the extraordinary elements on this planet that make a beautiful life possible. Most of the negative elements have been created by yourselves. If the higher realms had not been involved in the clearing and cleansing of your abuse, you would have already destroyed yourselves.

Through the balanced cosmic laws of giving and receiving, the more you give love and support to yourselves and the planet, the more you will receive.

Death has become an essential aspect of your life cycle due to the negative behavior of which you are capable. **Immortality can only be gifted to those who love and create, not destroy**. It is your destiny to return to love. Death is an escape from your present dense consciousness/behavior so you can return to your higher self and make another choice of what you would like/need to experience next time. Rethinking death as an opportunity to grow and expand can reduce your taught fear of it. For in truth you never die; you simply shift formats in order to learn what is necessary. Soon you will learn that you do not need to transition into other formats/forms. Through your raised consciousness you can choose to become an immortal being, your divine destiny.

Dear ones, take a deep breath and know all of which we speak is stored in your knowing heart. You can access it through your heart and us anytime you so choose.

WHAT WE CALL DEATH

Death is feared.
And yet ever so near.
Let us retrain ourselves
Through another view
And review a new view
Of what we call death.
Death is but an opportunity
For rest and reattunement,
To free us from the out-of-tunement,
Turmoil and imbalances of being Earth-bound,
Long enough to heal enough
To decide if we want another ride
On the physical side.

Perhaps physical format's only reason to be
Is for preparing, perfecting our human body
For another toddy, mixing and blending with its
Spiritual body, once again.

Maybe this reunion with spirit
Is the real reason for human experience,
At all.

When a loved one has passed on
They are actually with their higher body consciousness,
Causing celestial bliss.

If we could only remember
Our body is only a wardrobe,
We wear for a moment,
Until we shed it,
To accept a better opportunity to bed,
A fuller moment.

It is the unknowing of these truths
Which hamper humanity and keep
Us in self-created chains of non-clarity.

We get stuck and refuse
To understand the true cycle of life,
Dragging ourselves into stiff with self-pity,
Breaking down our resistance,
Creating more persistence in the resistance,
And what we resist, persists.

It is the lack of knowing our
True spiritual composition
That keeps us in the position
Of lack and limitation.

Let us celebrate and emulate
The fact that we are eternal beings.
Who can never die,
And when we leave these bodies,
Which we have done thousands of times before,
We shall mourn never more,
Knowing we have gloriously returned home,
To decide what our next roam, ride and home,
Shall be.

CHAPTER 22

HOW TO CREATE PEACE ON EARTH

From Archangel Uriel, World Teacher and Guardian

Dear Beloved Peace-Filled Humans,
     There is so much separation, duality, and confrontation in your world due to your individual wounds and ego defenses mirroring out into your collective world. As has been taught many times before, all this is the result of your unloving relationship with self reflecting out into your thus also wounded world. The ascension shift (moving into a higher frequency of existence), as mentioned, will be a **personal peace process of inside out**, beginning with each one of you.

The chosen messenger whom we are coming through at this divine moment, like many others, is a brethren within an endeavor called the Angel News Network, with many of our various higher-realm teachings to assist you in *your individuated personal peace process. Can you receive and apply these teachings?*

*Ultimately, as has been explained to you many times, the intention, through the healed loving relationship with self, is **to create***

communities of equality, harmony, and balance throughout your world. Remember, dear ones, *the purpose of your planet is to learn to love.* As your history reveals, this has not been an easy process for you. It does not have to be this difficult, if you can simply learn to think with your heart, allowing your mental bodies to be in service to your heart that knows all of which we speak. All the learning from past lives is stored in the DNA of your heart and passed on lifetime after lifetime.

Let us now examine how aspects of your higher selves can be applied to achieve the needed peace on your planet. **It is your destiny during the creation of your final golden age to learn to live together in peace through all your chosen diversity. Through your diversity, you are learning you are all aspects of the same thing: LOVE.**

Acknowledge the divine right of each and every person on Earth to be free of his or her wounds and defenses and reveal his or her higher selves; you are in the process of this. Learn how to champion each other's higher self through speaking your truth, knowing your needs, and set-ting your boundaries. This will allow the opportunity to awaken the full activation of your soul plans, your reason to be here. You each have talents and gifts to bring into world service, knowing the world would be incomplete without each of you. You are all aspects of the Creator experiencing itself. Be and do this with complete acceptance, compas-sion, and forgiveness as to how you have chosen to learn.

Remember, through your personal process, to have no hidden agenda or outcome other than the highest good of all. *Surrendering to not knowing* will allow the probabilities and pos-sibilities of the universe to come forth. This requires a quiet-ing of the mental body that constantly needs to know. Again, return to the source of your knowing heart. **Surrendering to not knowing allows the higher self to work.**

Dear ones, the peace you so hunger for can and will manifest in your lives, the lives of others, and your world if you simply apply the above words into action. Select world leaders (governments reflect the people they govern) who have evolved enough to apply these principles, and trust and know there are forces higher than humanity who are available to support you through your process. Seriously consider being in service to these forces; after all, they created you and all your past golden ages, and if you so choose, your next golden age.

ASCENDED MASTERS, AMONGST US

Ascended masters are always amongst us,
Guardians and gifts of humanity,
Who have worked many millennia
From the unseen to the seen

They enlighten and brighten and lift
Humanity out of our self-created
Self-centered creations.
These higher beings' domain
Is beyond death's doors,

Having eternal dominance
Over the physical body and terrain.

All things obey their command,
As they demand the laws of nature,
And the universe is at their converse.

CHAPTER 23

HUMAN SEXUALITY AND LOVE

From Archangel Uriel, World Teacher and Guardian

Dear Loving and Sexual Human Beings,
What love and your sexuality are has eluded you for eons. When you lost your direct higher-realm connections from whence you came, *you lost your true connection to the purpose of love and sexuality. In advanced civilizations love and sexuality are direct expressions of your divinity*. It is your destiny to reclaim this. What you now have experienced with both is but a shadow of the true reality of love and sexuality. In golden ages past, you did experience the divine connection of the *building block of love* and the human connection of your divine *erotic life force energies you call sexuality*. The time has come to recapture unconditional love and know the purpose of sexuality. It isn't what you have been taught and may think.

As you are waking up more and more, let us remember together the meaning, value, and purpose of love and human sexuality. **Love is not just an emotion felt, and**

sexuality is not just about your gender, reproduction, or with whom or where you place your genitals. Your corrupted, unloving relationships with self, others, and your world through distorted teachings in religions, cultural beliefs, and governments are now fully enforced in your definition and experiences of what you call love and sexuality. **Love and sexuality are essential elements that hold your world and universe together** and are here to **bring you great joy**, not what they now often bring you. How often have your present experiences of love and sexuality brought you joy and fulfillment, dear ones? They have often created feelings of control, sadness, and suffering in your lives.

There have been volumes written and spoken on these topics, but let us see if we can bring further clarity through a brief understanding of the **meaning, value, and purpose of love and sexuality** in your lives.

Suffice it to say, you do not yet fully comprehend the purpose of love, how to manifest with it, nor understand that sexuality is far more complex than two genders, heterosexual, or same-sex expressions. Since you are remembering that you are Oneness with ALL THERE IS, there are many diversified ALL THERE IS expressions of that Oneness. For instance, soon you will be ready to learn there are multiple expressions of gender reflecting the multiverse.

It is the fear of the full expression of how powerful and multidimensional you are that causes you to create your small boxes containing love and sexuality. Your chosen journey has been about self-empowerment and self-realization, a journey with many twists and turns. While the chains of untruth remain strong, it is your divine right to know truth. The veils between untruth and truth are very thin now due to the ascension process your planet and humanity are experiencing. Your 3-D illusion world is dissolving, as the old paradigm of duality dies—replaced by the new paradigm of paradise on Earth.

There are many courses of study available, such as the one we come to you through now, THE ANGEL NEWS NETWORK, which will assist you in unraveling the mysteries of life and the universe. We teach and know that the soul does exist and lives throughout eternity, and your sexuality and love are portions of this immortal aspect of you. **Your sexuality is a component of your love-force energy that maintains and sustains your desire to be here.** The expression of this *has no limit in what you call gender*; it is the diversified ways creation wishes to express itself (like the many life forms on your planet). Your fear of this truth has created your small definitions of what you call love and sexuality. A divine expression of love through sexuality can never be anything less than a true expression of God expressing itself.

Remember, dear ones, **the purpose of planet Earth is to learn to love**. How often have you shamed, blamed, and judged a loving sexual expression as a result of an unloving relationship with self and others? Please know that responsibility comes with this. In advanced civilizations, individuals are allowed full loving sexual expression while being taught how to prepare themselves for parenthood. There are no children having children. Much of your existing sexual behaviors today are between individuals attempting to fill an empty hole due to a lack of love.

As the consciousness of humanity increases, most of the negative consequences you now experience with love and sexuality will no longer exist. As you *advance into your multidimensionality* and sustain a direct connection from whence you came, **love and sexuality will take on cosmic consciousness**. The effort needed now is to keep your heart open to receive the many answers to your questions.

In order for you to receive from higher realms and for you to be able to apply it, you must trust and surrender to what is given. If there is not a balance of giving and receiving, the journey becomes more arduous. Allow your resonance and discernment to connect with the higher realms that are here to love and support you, dear ones. **Being ready to commit to receive is crucial**. Are you ready?

As many of you have learned, humans have been given more than your physical senses. It is your additional **higher telepathic senses where love and your sexuality truly reside and express themselves.** *And they have become quite creative in how they do that!* You see examples of that in your many "unaccepted" or not mainstream love and sexual expressions, which you are in the process of accepting with compassion. You are slowly beginning to see they are all expressions of the same Oneness.

All of which we speak at this time is a wisdom already stored in your heart that you are learning how to access and listen to. How do you do this, dear ones? By simply asking your higher self (soul) to support you. Ask and ye shall receive.

Dear ones, look into the mirror and ask yourself: What is keeping me from reclaiming my power and speaking my truth, stating my needs, and setting my boundaries?

It is time to know that love and your sexuality are your fullest expression of God being you, and you being God expressing itself divinely; that your love and sexuality is a way to join your divine higher selves with another and to reflect that out into the world.

Love and your sexuality are alive and well within your heart. They are the empowerment of the multiverse forever. You humans have often distorted both, turning them into something they are not. It is time to trust and know, and create a healthy relationship with love and sexuality that reflects your love of self.

During your many lifetimes you have been required to forget your true divine beingness. This allowed you to experience life more fully. This is also one of the reasons you have not yet awakened to the more expansive nature of love and sexuality. IT IS TIME TO ASK THAT THE VEILS OF FORGETFULNESS BE REMOVED. Then you will know more about love and sexuality than you ever thought possible. What you see now is the tip of the iceberg waiting to melt to join in oneness.

SERVICE

What does it mean to be
In true service to another?

What we think is service to all,
May not be service a' tall.

What many people consider service
Is mostly loss of self in others.
The act of satisfying and gratifying
The limitations of self,
Is not service.

This is the denigration of spirit,
And a dramatic demonstration of our
Lack and limitation.

The first and true service of anyone
Is the love and support of
The God-force within you,
The great master servant of self,
And teacher of everyone.

During our service to another,
If we hold our attention other than on
The Inner Source and Force Within,
We shall never win,
We shall move from servant to slave.

For when we possess this Inner-Force,
We can fully serve another,
Through having served self first.

For true service can only come
By embracing the master within,
That allows us to balance,
Giving and receiving, out and in.

Let us beware that our service to others,
Is not an excuse,
To strut our stuff,
In the presence of others.

CHAPTER 24

I DON'T LIKE YOU, BUT I LOVE YOU

What causes us not to like someone and yet feel a deep love for him or her?

The not liking comes from experiencing the **ego defenses** created around the **wounds** within the other, *fully expressed*. Through also seeing these within yourself, you can accept or reject them, experiencing a liking or not. (There are many teachings available on wounds and ego defenses in chapter 16, and/or connect with www.theangelnewsnetwork.com for more tools if needed.)

The pathway to move beyond the **not liking to love** is seeing and knowing that the other is not his/her wounds and defenses. Then you can choose to transcend them to the higher self of unconditional love.

By establishing, through self-love, your **truth, needs, and boundaries** around the other's wounds and defenses, you are able to maintain and sustain unconditional love. (For more teachings on truth, needs, and boundaries, see the website noted above.)

All of this not liking and love is simply a way we have chosen to learn to love: the reason we are here!

A PERFECT PERSON

Inside each of you
Lives a perfect person,
Who knows exactly
The right thing to be and do,
During all actions.

This perfect person,
Knows full well
Right from wrong,
And how to be strong
In the right well come.

Your perfect person
Is ready to leave
Their comfort zone
Of Being wrong,
And assist someone
Who is not so strong?

When this happens,
Magic manifests,
And you can rest assured,
And know,
You've allowed someone else to grow.

CHAPTER 25

IMPECCABILITY OF THE WORD

From Archangel Uriel, World Teacher and Guardian

Dear Humans of the World we love and support,
Your word, *the word,* is the most powerful gift given to humanity and is the *tool of Creation*. It is time you remember this truth, if you so choose.

At this time within your planetary and personal processes, the distortion and abuse of your/the word, the **nonimpeccability of your/the word, has become an invasive and pervasive destructive force in your lives**. Can you see (the consequence) the world of duality/separation/confrontation your behavior creates? Would you like to choose another choice?

Your word is a reflection/mirroring of your relationship with self. Are you having a loving relationship with yourself? Since it has become a *"cultural norm"* to speak untruths regularly, your highest good and soul plan (reason to be here) are not being supported.

As a result of your often accepting the nonimpeccability of the word, you are being *controlled by others*; **you are giving your power away**. The word is creation that is the power bestowed upon you. **Through the abuse of the word, how you deliver the word, and your freedom of choice and will, you have created the world you have now.**

Dear ones, you can begin to make another choice, to accept the power of the word that reflects your soul plans, divinity, and create a world of equality, harmony, and balance. **When there is not responsibility for the impeccability of the word and how you deliver it, your consequence is what you see now in your personal and planetary lives.**

Can you accept with compassion *how powerful you are?* This is a core issue, dear ones. Do you love yourself enough to reflect that out into your world? There are no mandates here. **You will learn from your choices until you make another choice.**

Dear ones, begin to hold yourself, your government, religions, and corporate leaders accountable to the impeccability of the word. Demand it; create a consequence when it is not honored.

It is your destiny and divine right to create a new world of oneness. If you so choose, allow **your word to reflect your divinity in its delivery and truth**. This is another core issue for you. What do you choose?

AUTHENTICITY AND INTEGRITY

Where did authenticity,
And integrity,
Go?

Did they run away because
They have no place to go or be?
Was it because the we got lost.
In the me?

In advanced civilizations
Everyone is telepathic,
So transparency prevents deceit,
And all meet in authentic celebrity.

The governments, religions and corporations
That think they control the world
Are lacking truth, and stacking untruths,
Aplenty.

People often say one thing,
And do another,
Confounding and confusing even one another.

There is much deceit,
And denial of that deceit,
Keeping us incomplete.

Truth is,
Governance is more effective
When we truly care,
And wish to share the truth.

None of us has all the answers,
Let's simply ask what others need,
And execute deeds
Of the highest good of all.

Let us leave the old paradigm
Of fear, greed, and control,
And mold a new reality
Based on authenticity and integrity,
And finally leave the old.

CHAPTER 26

YOU ARE NOT HERE TO DESTROY NOR ENSLAVE

*From Archangel Uriel, World Teacher and
Guardian, and Gaia, Mother Earth*

Dear Beloved Children of Earth,

All conscious life—minerals, plants, animals, and you—are *made of the same sacred stuff/elements*: the same atoms, electrons, etc. You are all here to evolve within your soul plans and to support and love one another. That does not include killing one another or enslaving one another.

Each living conscious being on your planet came here from various galaxies and worlds, and chose to be here to support the evolutionary process of this particular planet. **The mission of this planet is to learn to love**. Love is the building block of the universe, dear ones. All beings within this world have freedom of choice and will, and are not here by random accident or by an imaginary evolutionary process.

The present relationship animals are having with one another (eating each other) **reflects humanity's**

corrupted relationship with self. It was not always that way and need not be in the future. When humanity returns into a higher frequency of consciousness, animals will return in behavior to reflect their divinity. At present, **there are more humans enslaved, in bondage, than ever before**. This continued behavior **reflects your disconnection with your divinity and purpose in being here** (to learn to love). How much more pain and suffering do you need to learn to free yourselves and ascend into an existence of oneness? We higher realms are giving you many teachings and tools to assist your awakening. Once you understand the truth of how and why your world was created, you will never return to your old paradigm again; **you are in process, dear ones**. This is the way you chose to learn. Accept it with compassion and forgive it, and begin to make another choice, if you so choose.

Throughout your distorted relationship with self, your planet, and all life upon it, humanity has created abuses that must stop in order for you to advance as a species, or you will destroy yourselves (again). **All of you are needed to make this unique, extraordinary experiment of diversity called planet Earth work!**

Dear ones, within advanced higher-frequency civilizations (some on your planet), animals, plants, and minerals are not destroyed or *enslaved as pets*. This may be difficult for some to understand, since they see themselves as more advanced or better than animals, plants, and minerals. Dear humans, these conscious beings have more innate abilities than you do through their direct connection to Source. They are not meant to be destroyed nor enslaved by humanity. Humanity has attempted to conquer even nature and has learned this thinking does not work. **You are intended to be in divine service to one another that does not include death or enslavement.**

You are all here to be in WORLD SERVICE to one another, your planet, and the forces that created, maintain, and sustain you. Rather basic reasons to be here, from which you have long separated yourselves, and from one another.

It is time to know and remember all your soul plan reasons to be here and support one another. You simply **cannot survive without the complete cooperation of one another.** Through your narcissism and ego, you have created much cruelty to the other life forms and yourselves that reflect your relationship with self.

No other life form is meant to be at the will or under the control of another. You are in stewardship to one another. You all have freedom of choice and will to be here. Just because you do not know this or believe this does not mean it does not exist. You have and will continue to experience severe consequences by not waking up to this truth.

Dear ones, you can coexist, respecting each other's divine soul plans and need to interact, without killing or enslaving one another. You can enjoy the "fruits" of other life forms without destroying them. **This is how advanced civilizations act.**

You can eat the apple without killing the tree. **This new awareness will prepare you for interacting with other species from other worlds in your near future.**

Through greed you have altered the genes of many plant and animal species, attempting to control their life cycle and their ability to survive without you. Similar experiments took place on Atlantis and ended in disaster. In effect, this is a form of self-sabotage, for when you ingest these "creations" you are altering your own genes.

Advanced civilizations reflect the degree to which they honor and treat all life forms, knowing all is divine and needed. As mentioned earlier, humanity's insanity has even included attempts to control nature itself. You have learned that does not serve you or your planet well; in fact, it can mean your destruction if you continue it. **There are forces beyond your wisdom** that support nature and you, dear ones. It is your destiny to again be connected to them.

Humanity is showing signs of great progress in waking up, but there are forces still attempting to keep you in *a dense state of destruction.*

Dear ones, we realize you need to eat and survive within the 3-D world you choose to be in. But we caution you to examine the ways you attempt to do this. There are planetary **karmic consequences** when your planet and all within and upon her body are not honored.

There are new energy technologies being revealed to you where you can create all you need without greed or threat to others, especially your home planet. These new technologies will require a restructuring of your economic and governmental systems, creating We Consciousness, not Me Consciousness.

Humanity does not own the life forces of creation. It is time humanity's ego moves into service to your heart that knows this truth. *Reconnecting with and being in service to the forces of creation are essential next steps. This process will allow the creation of your next and final golden age.*

While there appears to be a loving relationship between humans and their pets or work animals, it is a form of enslavement that reflects your ability to enslave one another through an unhealed relationship with self. No species, including yours, wishes to sacrifice its freedom of will. There are ways to support one another through a deep awareness and honoring of the other life forms that reflects a healed relationship with self.

Trees and plants are here to be the planet's lungs, supplying oxygen, and protecting your planet from the weather your thoughts and emotions create. Minerals are the nervous system of the planet. Many animal species are the guardians of the planet from other star systems. Many species have left the planet due to humanity's abuse and returned to their home galaxies, what you call extinction. **Dear ones, you need to understand the purpose of each of you being here and how interdependent you all are. This is going to be an essential next step in your ascension/evolutionary process.**

It is time to let go of the concept that you can control nature or other life forms. *You did not create them, and you cannot control them.* The life forms that remain on the planet are vital to your survival, whether you understand this or not. *Your ignorance can be your undoing; your wisdom your pathway to eternity.* All chose to be here for a purpose. **An important part of your journey on this planet is discovering this truth**. You are all divine beings created from the same elements. Communities of equality, harmony, and balance can reflect this truth.

If you so choose, wake up, humanity, and know that all life is precious and sacred; it is not yours to destroy or to enslave. You have all chosen to be a part of a divine experiment called the "Lover-versity" of Earth. Once you truly learn to love self and all others, you will go forward to become the master teachers of other worlds, your destiny.

BALANCE OF GIVING AND RECEIVING

The grand balance of life
Is maintained and sustained
By giving and receiving.
Here's the deal,
We cannot receive without giving,
And we cannot give without receiving,
In real.

How do you feel about this deal?
Does it seem real, in your life?

Many have been taught
It's better to give than receive
But this is a bit of a deceive.

If you don't receive in balance
Within what you give,
You soon lose the energy or desire to give.
Thus, no balance to live.

This bewitching balance
Is based upon loving self enough
Not to leave self-love on the shelf, of life.

To achieve this birthing balance,
We speak our truth,
Define our needs,
And set some boundaries,
In order to relieve, at lack of balance.

Do you know your truth?
Who you are and why you are here?
Do you know your needs?
Or are they stuck in the weeds, of life?
And last but not least,
Have you set boundaries in all relations?
So balance can bring full elations?

There are many rules and tools,
Once again revealed to man
To support you in knowing when, what and where
And how to stand,
Through who and why, in balance.
For without balance,
We fall off the soul plan beam,
And into the stream of imbalance,
And possible malice.

CHAPTER 27

DOES YOUR EDUCATION NEED EDUCATING?

From the Archangelic Realm of Uriel

Dear Beloved Humans with whom we are in service,
    At this crucial time within your evolutionary path, let us now discuss knowledge and wisdom, and how many are not actually educating your youth, and yourselves, **by not knowing the truth of your existence**. In reality, you have largely not known your past and how you have arrived at your present. There have been advanced civilizations for millions of years on this planet, and none of you originated from here. Soon this will become common truth and a game-changer in your world.

*During much of your past and within your present education systems, your teaching methods have largely been affected by the masculine-mind, assertive energy. You have been "telling" your students and self what it is you think you **know**, and asking them to repeat this back to you. And if they do not, they will not succeed. This "knowledge" has not led to **wisdom** (accumulated truth that can be used in the present and future). Look at your world now. There is no applied wisdom! Much* *of what you think you know is not truth, nor does it serve the needs (highest good) of your students or yourselves, dear ones. In fact, there has been very little truth within your world. Much of the truth has been concealed from you by the forces that have attempted to control you for eons (religions, governments, educational institutions, cultural belief-values, and corporations). This is all in the process of quickly changing.*

Your students and yourselves need your souls (and soul plans) fed at this time, not just your minds, dear ones. By experiencing your soul plan, you will know who you are and why you are here. You really do not understand the construction of what you call your mind, or how the brain really works. Since the *believing* mind is finally returning in service to the *truthful* heart, this is a wonderful opportunity to revisit the entire concepts of knowing, wisdom, education, and truth. And what your soul, your eternal aspect, really needs at this time—and this is **truth** that will set you free from yourselves.

The heart actually contains all the knowledge you have accumulated from your past lives and allows this to be accessed through your discernment and resonance into present wisdom. Of course, another missing ingredient for many in humanity is knowing that you have had many lifetimes on this planet (another truth intentionally kept from you). Dear ones, it makes no sense that you merely have one life. Through your many lifetimes, you have experienced all you came here to experience in order to ascend into immortal beings of service to the forces that created you.

The challenge for humanity is to know that most of your wisdom and your movement forward on your evolutionary path (which is your divine destiny) has been the result of stimulation and wisdom coming from outside the human mind.

From sources outside themselves, humans received the ideas, inventions, and gifts that have moved humanity forward. These were not created in your minds; they were received through the *divine dance of giving and receiving* (which you are learning to balance now). The mind and others have wanted you to believe that it is *all there is*—and **ALL THERE IS**, is beyond the human mind, dear ones. Can you accept this truth, and your need to maintain and sustain connection to these higher realms whose intention is to support and love you? And assist in moving you into another golden age of equality, harmony, and balance.

This cosmic **consciousness of which we speak** can change the entire concept of what we call wisdom and true education, and where information and truth reside, if you so choose. **Cosmic consciousness knocks the ego of the "educated" back into its unknowing**. By surrendering to the "unknowing" you open all possibilities and probabilities, dear ones. What is called the void is the foundation of creation; from nothing all things come. Once you can subdue (not eliminate) the human mind within educating yourselves, you can come to know truth. And that truth can set you free from all lack and limitation. **The human mind can be a wonderful vehicle for moving this (new) truth forward; not saying it is the source.**

Let your teachers become students and your students become teachers, and vice versa again, dear ones. For in truth, all the wisdom each of you needs to know resides within each and every one of you. You are simply learning how to access it. This will begin to feed your soul and bring joy into your awakening experience. For you are really not learning, you are

simply awakening what innately lives within each of you. You see this in nature most often with your animals and plants, dear ones. Follow their example and be at peace.

This awakening is meant to be **free to all**. There is no need to accumulate student loan debt and joylessly memorize facts (that can change) that simply continue to imprison you, dear ones. Each one of you has an internal gyro system, your resonance and discernment, which will allow you to know what you need to awaken within you. Your joy will show you the path. This is how advanced civilizations experience life and learning, dear ones. We await you following this example.

The cyberspace communication technology that we have gifted you is meant to further assist your awakening and learning—your true education. Yes, dear ones, we gifted it to you. Someone did not invent it. But there are plenty abusing it and profiting from it. Again, many of your so-called inventions were received from higher realms to advance your evolution (creating the golden ages of the past). The sooner humanity knows and accepts this truth, the faster your advance will be and the more joyful your world will become.

Many of your educational institutions are in transition at present, realizing much of what used to work no longer does, but not knowing which way to turn. Some are holding on to the old way of being to the death. Let the teaching and reminders here allow you to create a new paradigm in learning, to access wisdom and bring more joy and truth into your lives like never before.

WISDOM

Be not proud of your wisdom,
Those who think you know it all.
For confidence is just an ego defense
Of the wounded child not feeling good at all,
Being left out on the fence.

Discourse with the ignorant and the wise,
For in reality, we are all simply teaching
What we need to learn, and prize.

If some looking shallow
Comes to you full of knowledge,
Listen and heed
For wisdom has no greed.

CHAPTER 28

OWNERSHIP

From Archangel Uriel, World Teacher and Guardian

D ear Beloved Humans becoming self-empowered,
Only through taking *ownership* of everything that happens (*that you manifest*) in your lives can you *free yourself from victimhood: the shaming, blaming, and judging of self and others.*

There are no accidents or other events that take place in your life that do not include your freedom of choice and will. Your freedom of choice and will is a grand gift from creation that no one can take from you (many have tried on and off this planet, to no avail); that's **how powerful you are, dear ones.**

All of the events in your past and present lives are the *not-so-simple ways* you have chosen to learn what you needed to learn to fulfill your destiny (soul plan) to become the master teachers of the universe.

The reason many of your existing therapies do not release you from addiction, what you call abuses, and other so-called *negative* events is because they do not include your ownership, your self-empowerment of your lives.

Dear ones, we understand that the truth/reality we speak of may be challenging for many of you. But only through your acceptance with compassion, thus forgiveness, as to how you have chosen to learn can you free yourselves from yourselves.

You are not here to be victims or punished. You are here to advance in your evolutionary path to fulfill the embodiment of your divinity. The forces from whence you came simply do not punish or include victimhood.

By choosing to become human, you agreed to experience all that you have through your many lifetimes. The healing of these experiences is taking place at this rare opportunity of ascension (raising your consciousness and vibration into a higher realm of existence).

Dear ones, nothing can happen in your life without your agreement. In taking ownership of this truth you assume the responsibility, and the consequence is self-empowerment and *freedom from judgment*.

*Take a deep breath and connect with your heart that knows all of which we speak. Your ownership of everything in your life is an essential teaching at this time, to welcome your eternal beingness. The inclusion of this truth is **a vital missing link in your consciousness/awareness.***

As beings who came here from various worlds to be a unique part of this divine experiment called Earth, whose mission is to learn to love, you are the Creator experiencing all aspects of itself. You have agreed to move as far from this truth as possible in order to learn what you needed to learn. It was the only way you could learn it. It is time to journey back home, and to know and remember who you are and why you are here. Now you are readying yourself to apply your wisdom here and elsewhere.

Dear ones, you no longer have to fear your true sense of self, your divinity and power. Now you are awakening to the world and the universe.

As your old-time religions say, "Free again, at last, thank God Almighty, free again at last!"

SELF-MASTERY

See if you can never be surprised,
Nor taking things personally,
Nor not raised,
By the prize.

Dominion of self, at all times,
Allows the rhythm of life to manifest,
To rhyme.

Only by balancing of self
Can Self-Mastery be tested and bested,
Maintained and sustained,
Through no electricity but elasticity.

Be sure nothing from you is less than your best,
While not allowing a

Negative word or deed
To proceed.

All forces in the universe
Are waiting your command
Through the right use of tongue and hand.

The All-Controlling God-force
Lives deep within you,
Do not forget to use it and be true.

CHAPTER 29

PEACE IS A PLANET CALLED LOVE

From Archangel Uriel, World Teacher and Guardian

Dear Be-LOVE-ed Humans,
In order to have **peace**, you need to have **love**, the foundation of ALL THERE IS. In order to have love, you need **forgiveness (forgiving how you chose to learn).** In order to have forgiveness, you need **acceptance and compassion**. So our **ingredients of peace are: love, acceptance, compassion, and forgiveness.**

What if we were to explain to you that *love did not originate on this planet*; in fact, none of you did. You all gathered here from elsewhere in the universe to create a **learning laboratory of love**. The reason, dear ones, you have not yet achieved peace on your now home planet is due to the reality that you have not yet achieved love—the key component of peace. You have gotten as far from love and peace as you can possibly get without destroying yourselves. You are reaching a point of critical mass again. Are you ready to turn back in the other direction toward your hearts and return to the frequency and vibration of **love (the purpose of this planet)** in order to achieve peace?

As you traveled from various galaxies and solar systems to join here on the Lover-versity campus called planet Earth, **your first stop was the planet Venus, the planet of love**, where you downloaded the DNA of unconditional love. You lived on Venus for many millennia prior to transporting the unconditional love DNA into the heart core of planet Earth. This allowed you to pioneer the planet. You have directly connected with this love DNA during past Earth golden ages, but lost your connection each time for various abusive reasons. Now you are again seeing the opportunity to activate and **connect with the frequency of love, nestled inside the core of your planet, through a process called ascension.**

Only through your learned love of self can you and your planet achieve everlasting peace. This is why your planet remains in a nonpeaceful situation within your nations and worldwide.

You cannot and will not achieve world peace until you heal the wounds and defenses within each of you. Many higher realms have gifted humanity with teachings and tools throughout the eons to assist you. Are you ready to apply them? Are you ready to heal your wounds and defenses created from a lack of love? How much more unnecessary suffering do you need to endure through your freedom of choice and will?

The megahertz frequency from the core of your planet is radiating out the vibration of love. This frequency maintains and sustains your heartbeat. Place your hand upon your heart now and connect with that energy of love. **Each beat of your**

heart is a reminder that you are love. When will you be able to receive this love, know you are lovable, and reflect that out into your world through peace?

With love and peace as the tools, you can and will create communities of equality, harmony, and balance. You can graduate from the Lover-versity and take your diploma of love and peace out into world and universal service.

Dear ones, over the eons you have simply been asleep and forgotten that you are love and peace. It is time to wake up! We higher realms simply wish to remind and stimulate you in remembering who you are and why you are here. We wish nothing more than for you to take your eternal/immortal place at the table of love and peace as the powerful, loving beings you are.

When you first came to this planet, you lived in *harmonic resonance* with the frequency of love and peace. Together, we received and gave the essence of love and peace, **a state of being you are remembering now**. Go deeply into your heart's memory banks and see what memories you can feel. Each member of Earth knew the reason he/she came here, to learn to fully be love. This love created a Oneness that radiated out to all elements of the planet.

This civilization of love and oneness has not been recorded in your history books, since no one was left to remember or write about it. **This is why we are telling this story now, dear ones.** Now you can remember and re-create.

Your ancestors are love and peace beings, and they were capable of creating golden ages beyond your imagination or abilities now. The time when you truly existed as One, through love and peace, is upon you again now—a time to create a final golden age.

As we mentioned, all of which we speak is stored within your heart and the Universal Halls of Wisdom. Your memory of loving and peaceful communities embedded in your hearts can now be brought forth in your consciousness and create a new world paradigm: communities of equality, harmony, and balance.

What is holding you back from love and peace now is the unhealed relationship with self. **The unhealed *me* needs to decidedly move back into service to the *healed we consciousness*.** We have given you many tools and teachings to achieve this (personal processing and cyber technologies). Are you ready to apply them? Or do you wish to keep seeking and continue the world you have now?

Fear, the absence of love, has controlled the minds and hearts of humanity long enough. People wander the Earth not knowing who they are (divine beings having a human experience, preparing to becoming the master teachers of the universe) or why they are here (to learn to love as a tool of creation).

Dear ones, you are capable of manifesting all of which we speak. It is time to wake up before you actually destroy yourselves. You can choose to work together as peaceful, loving sisters and brothers, all needing the same things, made of the same elements. Imagine the probabilities and possibilities that peace and love can bring.

Connect your hearts, dear ones; speak lovingly to one another; care about yourself and planet equally; begin to know the power that love and peace can create and how you can put it to best use. Remember, **the love from whence you came is stored inside your own heart right now.**

LOVE AND LIGHT

The Light is God's way
Of creating and maintaining and sustaining
Peace and Perfection through Creation.
It is the way of showing us
The clear Light of day.

The transcendent and magnificent
Actives of Love and Light
Are the ways to show us
Our manifested might.

Man never ceases creating
Through love and light, his God-Self.
Transcending the little self-elf,
Of lacking and limiting.

Let us choose to live
At the Center of our Being
In light and love,
Surpassing any surgery of the soul.

Light forgives all mistakes
Of the human self.
Acceptance and compassion
Is all that it takes?

CHAPTER 30

THE PURPOSE OF RELATIONSHIPS

Inspired by Archangels Gabriel, Michael, Raphael, and Uriel

Dear Beings learning to love self,
   More and more, as a human species, you are understanding and knowing the universal truth: **the only relationship you are having is the one with yourself, and you can only love others to the degree you love yourself.** There are many teachings within the Angel News Network (see Life Mastery, www.theangelnewsnetwork.com, channeled materials and books) and elsewhere to support a loving relationship with you that can then reflect and mirror out into the world around you. **If you better understand and know the meaning, value, and purpose of relationships mirroring self, you just might increase the success of them.** Then you can more fully embrace and embody their divine purpose in your lives: to create communities of equality, harmony, and balance.

How you feel about yourself, thus others, is taught. You are not born not loving yourself and one another. Now you can begin a new teaching and create a new you through the support of higher realms that love you unconditionally, until you can fully love one another and yourselves. Then you will create a world that reflects who you truly are: divine beings.

GROWTH AND EXPANSION

As you learn more about yourself through your *wounds and ego defenses*, you become more conscious and your original wounding can begin to heal. Through *personal processes* you can learn more about how your chosen maturation-family situations created unmet needs. Through the "*ownership*" of the choices you made, you can become responsible for what it is you chose to learn and how you chose to learn it. This moves you **from victimhood to self-empowerment**. You begin to know that **life is a process of inside out, not outside in**. You realize the other person is not there to fulfill what you can yourself. This prevents codependency.

You begin to know that the purpose of each relationship you are having is for your own growth and expansion, reflecting what is happening throughout the universe. For the universe would be incomplete without each and every one of you.

SEEING THE ILLUSIONS OF RELATIONSHIPS

You have so many illusions, and sometimes delusions, associated with your teachings around relationships. In fact, there is very little truth within your concepts and ideas of what relationships truly are. Through the taught shaming, blaming, and judging of self, you do the same to others.

One of the first truths to integrate is that your parents are responsible for your well-being. They are here **to nurture first so you may learn** what you came here to learn. Often your parents focus on what you are not, thus creating the shaming and blaming that you need to release (the reason you chose it). When a parent or someone else says, "I must change you," you have a choice to take responsibility for yourself and see the parent as the needed mirror. Isn't it fascinating how the universe works and how you choose to learn? If you so choose, you learn that no one else is here to make you feel whole and safe. That is your responsibility, and when you do not assume it, you experience the consequence of that choice. When you've had enough consequences, you make another choice.

SPEAK YOUR TRUTH, NEEDS, AND BOUNDARIES

In order to know your truth, it is essential to know who you are and why you are here, two questions that you seldom ask yourselves or are asked by others. The "who" and the "why" in your lives defines your purpose. Your purpose is fueled by your passion, how you feel and resonate. From higher realms there are many teachings at present to assist humanity through a personal process of determining who you are and why you are here, if you need assistance. (See Life Mastery, www.the-angelnewsnetwork.com.) It is not unusual for many of you not to know your needs, or for them to get lost within the needs of others. How often have others asked you, "What do you need?" When was the last time a needy child asked his/her parents if they needed anything? It is important to know you have real needs, for if your needs are not satisfied, it reduces your ability to support others.

It sounds simple, but the best way to satisfy your needs is to know them and communicate them to others.

Communicate your needs as a preference, not as a command or demand, which can create resistance to them. Be conscious of the negative egos, and attempt not to use manipulation as a way to get what you want, not what you need. This is a substitute for unmet needs.

Your boundaries allow the best use of your energy and what serves your highest good. Always ask yourselves these two questions in setting your boundaries: "Is this the best use of my energy, and is this serving my highest good?" Take a deep breath and go into your knowing heart for the response. Your resonance and discernment will assist greatly in establishing boundaries. Like needs, many of us don't know we can have boundaries.

NEEDS OF THE OTHER

Many do not realize that a relationship is a wonderful opportunity to provide the needs of the other person—be it wife, husband, lover, brother, sister, mother, father, or pet. It's about the universal law of balancing giving and receiving (which can be a challenge). If giving without the need to get and receiving without the need to give are organically achieved, these can become a great opportunity to learn giving and receiving. When the other's needs become as important as your own, this will be a strong non-codependent relationship. When you express your needs freely, and give without thought of self, a process of healing inner wounds and ego defenses also is achieved through the positive energy exchanged.

VALUE TALENTS AND GIFTS EQUALLY

Each person has unique talents and gifts to offer the world. In fact, the universe would be incomplete without all these. There are many personal processes to assist others in knowing their talents and gifts, if they are not presently aware of them (see Life Mastery, www.theangelnewsnetwork.com). Bring these out into world service reflecting your self-love and value of the other person; know these are fragments of both of your divine soul plans. Give equally, more than you expect to receive, and see what happens. When you have gratitude for what you do receive, true abundance comes.

PERSONAL GROWTH AND EXPANSION

When you realize all relationships are for your own personal growth and expansion, your consciousness shifts greatly. Through your ownership of the relationships you bring into your lives (with truth, needs, and boundaries), everyone becomes a reflection or mirror of yourself. You abandon victimhood for self-empowerment. You can regain the forgotten aspects of self and expand more into who you are and why you are here: activating your soul plan. Through this awareness, you can begin to relate to everyone and eliminate duality, separation, and confrontation (which are so active in the world today).

IN CONCLUSION

These tools are presented to assist you in freeing yourselves from yourselves in order to create a world of equality, harmony, and balance during the next golden age.

WE ARE ONE

As soon as we can realize
We're a collection of soul connections
Then duality and separation
Will be simply sent, away...

We shall know we are surely
One old soul
Who has never really
Been sold into separation.

The vicious veil of separation
Is finally to be lifted.
We're being released,
From duality,
That never had any reality.

We are One Divine Soul,
Old in our role,
Of consciousness and love.

Every creation molecule,
Knows it's all been a silly ridicule,
Until now.

CHAPTER 31

RESONANT CAUSATION AND CONSCIOUSNESS

How Does One Affect the Other?

From Archangel Uriel, World Teacher and Guardian

Dear Beloved Beings, being human,
What you resonate with causes you to become conscious of it and manifest it. Resonance often comes through as a result of your feelings. *Resonance and discernment* are mighty tools in pointing you in a direction that serves your highest good and that of others. Your **resonance** (*how you feel about it*) is within your **emotional body** that lives within your heart, and your *discernment* (*what you think about it*) lives within your **mental body**. Within your ascension process your mental body, powered by the assertive **masculine energy**, is moving *back into service to* the knowing/loving heart, empowered by the receptive **feminine energy**. *You are*

in the process of balancing the masculine and feminine energies. Can you better see why now?

Resonance is created when the frequency/vibration of a person, place, or thing is vibrating at a matched frequency to the other. The *synchronistic resonance* between the two feels pleasant, and actually activates your life force energy to live. This resonance can attract more of the same. **Your ability to be aware of the resonance is what awakens your consciousness, as you become further aware of what truly resonates for you.**

Resonance in effect becomes your truth; knowing what resonates and what does not. Through resonance you can better be able *to speak your truth, define you needs, and set your boundaries* in life. All this is reflecting self-love.

Resonance is a key component in creating communities of equality, harmony, and balance. A lack of resonance creates dissonance, duality, separation, and often conflict.

Resonance is an initial step within your ascension process, moving into higher frequencies of existence (your divine destiny). **This is the reason you have been gifted with resonant causation and consciousness.**

So resonance is like an internal gyro system, a gift from the gods, for you to know within your divine soul plan what is true for you and what serves your highest good, and perhaps the world, best.

Resonance actually creates a frequency around itself of which others can entrain. **You entrain to the highest frequency within the environment**. Resonance is actually creating your weather patterns and many natural events.

An excellent way to connect with your resonance is to become quiet and connect with your heart space, where your resonance resides. Allow your mental body (discernment) to more and more move into service to the heart. This process takes practice and commitment, but it is worth it, dear ones. Your heart knows all of which we speak. Your dormant telepathic abilities, your sixth sense, are alive and well inside your heart. When you quiet your other five senses and *do not make it about you*, a whole new realm of possibilities and probabilities comes forth from the void, the unknowing. This will allow you to access your own resonance and that of another more easily.

The application of your resonance and consciousness allows many wonder-filled moments in your life, such as:

* Connecting with like-spirited/like-minded people

* Connecting with higher-realm frequencies beyond the human mind and spirit

* Gaining wisdom beyond any knowledge that exists within you at present

* Expanding your soul plan through the application of your talents and gifts

* Better understanding who you are and why you are here

* Improving your well-being, health, and longevity with increased purpose

* Connecting the past and present into the now

* Having the secrets of life and the universe revealed in relation to your soul plan

The universe is an ever-growing and expanding being, and so are you. Your resonance and consciousness are tools gifted to you to fully activate your reason in being here. Now, if it resonates, share all you have learned with others and create a new world paradigm of love.

AN INTERNAL GYRO SYSTEM: RESONANCE

We have a gifted gyro system
In each of us.
It is a must that we use it,
Or we lose it,
And experience the consequence.

The system is called resonance.
It's how you feel about something,
To determine dissonance or not.

It is a vibrational frequency
Of a person, place or thing,
That will determine

If you have a similar ring,
Or frequency.

The ability to use resonance
Is a key component
In the moment of expanding
Your discernment, awareness and fairness.

CHAPTER 32

SPIRITUALITY SIMPLY SAID

From Archangels Gabriel and Uriel

Dear Spiritual Beings, being human,

At this crucial time in your planetary and personal transmutation into higher consciousness (the mission of the Angel News Network), it is essential that you know through your ability *to think with your loving heart*s what is actually happening, energetically and physically, and why.

From various choices you have made, you have been asleep for a long time. Now you are awakening and remembering, once again, who you are and why you are here. It is time to simply remember and know that you agreed to forget everything associated with your true identity so you would/could work your way back to your truth, so **you would never forget again**. It is time to understand and know your divinity; that you are the cocreator experiencing all aspects of the Creator. **Through the unconditional love of the Creator, your partner, you are now being freed (liberated) from the**

learning choices of separation and duality you made so long ago.

You imposed your forgetting upon yourselves as a result of your abuse of your divinity through thinking you could separate yourselves from the forces from whence you came, who maintain and sustain and love you. As a result, lifetime after lifetime, your souls have been downloaded with untrue belief systems about your partner, the Creator, and yourselves. These untruths still exist today in your religions, governments, and corporations who continue to attempt to control you. Now, through the true eyes of your divinity, you are finding your way back home.

The major factor that has also handicapped you is your ability to overcomplicate your spirituality, your divinity. This has been largely corrupted through the above untrue belief systems. In reality, there is little truth in your world today.

The higher realms teach you that true spirituality is a simple concept that you choose to complicate. **The fact is, it is so simple that you don't believe or know it, and have actually forgotten how to be spiritual and to embrace/embody it.**

The mental body loves to overcomplicate, especially things it does not fully understand (and that is most of reality). You see this throughout your educational systems; if they cannot see or prove it, it does not exist. Throughout your history there have been literally millions of books written about God and spirituality. How many of them have brought you closer to the truth? Few of these books, often written by spiritually unknowing people, know the simple truths that authentic spirituality offers. You still live in a world filled with separation and conflict as a result of not knowing the truth about your spirituality, your true essence.

TRUE SPIRITUALITY IS A STATE OF BEING, A PURE EMBODIMENT OF CONSCIOUSNESS THAT RETURNS YOU TO EQUALITY, HARMONY, AND BALANCE—YOUR DIVINITY.

Your spirituality is not based upon what you do or do not do, or the belief systems of your culture that are often your comfort zones. **Spirituality simply "IS" (I AM THAT I AM).** All the rituals, guidelines, habits, and patterns based upon do this, or do not do that, may be through well-meaning people, but rarely **infuse spirituality into your beingness**. You, as individuated aspects of creation, can and must do this alone in loving reunion with your spirituality, your divine essence (and who you truly are).

The purpose of this writing, as many within the Angel News Network, is to bring a higher-realm teaching into world service that is simple to know, and always bring you back to the God Power within, as the great Creator of our lives through the activation of your soul plans. (See *Man Power God Power* under books, www.theangelnewsnetwork.com, for an extended teaching.)

Let you now know and remember your spirituality, your divine essence, is alive and well within you, always ever ready to create the lives you say you want as divine beings.

LAW OF LOVE

When humanity finally finds the fortitude
To live with the everlasting Law of Love
We shall discover the release
From the cycle of birth and rebirth.
This will surely bring much mirth.

The reason and existence of humanity
Is to learn to love
Self, thus others, unconditionally.

Once this is finally in place,
The perpetual problems of the human race,
Will finally erase.

In problem's place will be
Ever expanding joy and truth
That forever creates fruitful youth.

With no blockages,
We shall then dock at
Constant new creations of what
Abides and builds in love.

Life is perpetual perfect motion
That neither sleeps nor slumbers,

And love is the sustaining stream
That means continuous creation.
When we succor self and are obedient
To the Laws of Love
The last enemy of man will be arrested,
Death will disappear,
And be dissolved in ever lasting
Life of love.

CHAPTER 33

TEN TENETS OF EARTH LIFE

(Cosmic Codes of Conduct)

From Archangel Uriel, World Teacher and Guardian

D ear Beloved Earth Beings,

(1) First and foremost, remember from whence you came. Be conscious of the forces that created you and maintain and sustain you; consider serving these forces as a priority in your life.

(2) Do not allow your emotions, thoughts, and actions to harm yourself or another. All harm returns to the provider in increased magnitude and caustic karma.

(3) Focus on creating a world of equality, harmony, and balance, joyfully loving all things. This can and will create a new you and new world paradigm.

(4) Allow your self-love to reflect out to the planet (your home) and others, thus keeping your wounds and ego defenses in check.

(5) Know that your body and the planet are sacred temples. Treat both with respect; the consequence of not being respectful of these is death.

(6) Begin to know, embrace, and embody the empowerment of simply being silent, being your message through resonance, creating peace on Earth.

(7) Know that heartfelt gratitude for "what is" creates abundance; reduce focusing on "what is not."

(8) Acceptance and compassion through forgiveness frees and empowers you and replenishes your world.

(9) Allow your emotions, thoughts, and words to reflect the life and world you say you want, for they do create everything around you.

(10) Know you are Creation experiencing itself. Know that each of you, your planet, and the cosmos are all interdependent.

AS ABOVE, SO BELOW

Look above, or below,
Whether you can see it or not,
Things are the same.
It's all part of the Oneness
That is the essence of the Oneness and Same,
Game.

Whether high or low consciousness
We're all on the same path
And shall arrive at the same destination,
No matter the math.

There are forces above and below,
Aplenty,
Sending wisdoms and love
To, we, in the middle,
Who have thought ourselves so little,
So long.

The time has come for the middle,
Above, below and not so little,
To join in the middle,
Once more.

Once we unite,
Things are going to get quite bright,
As legions of light and angels,
Dance with us in the middle, not so little.
When we unite with the bright light,
Our world service, and beyond
Begins and we shall experience
How truly mighty and grand our Soul plan,
Is.

Then, the "is" joins the I AM,
And we know I AM is who
I AM that I AM.

CHAPTER 34

THE GIFTS OF TECHNOLOGY:

Who Truly Owns and Controls A Natural Resource from Higher Realms?

From the Archangelic Realm of Uriel

Dear Beloved Human Sisters and Brothers,

We of the Archangelic Realm of Uriel come to you once again at this essential pathway position within your soul plan and destiny to speak to you about our gifts of technological communication advancement.

Several of your Earth years ago, we came to you through this channel to foretell the coming gifts of technical communication achievements, which many of you have now. We told the purpose of this was to assist you in transforming and freeing you from the many structures in your governments, religions, and corporations that continue to control you. Through fragments of his soul plan and synchronicity, this channel created a communication endeavor to introduce the personal computer to humanity. This is an update and continuation of our contacting humanity at this time. (The author produced an Apple Computer TV commercial that launched the personal computer age.)

As in previous advanced civilizations on your planet, there are currently imbalances and abuses of our gift, creating corruption, greed, and separation, which was never the intention of the gift. This reveals deep wounds continuing worldwide within humanity that need healing. Through revealing these wounds, not judging them, we are here to assist in creating frequencies to assist you in healing the imbalances within your emotional and mental selves. As in all healing, this is a process of inside out (not outside in), creating a breakdown followed by a breakthrough. Much of what you are experiencing throughout your lives and world is a breakdown of your controlling systems. It may appear things are getting worse. They are not. They are in process, and our technological communication gift is part of the solution, not the problem that many are creating from it, dear ones.

There have been and will continue to be teachings and tools from our realm and others to assist you. The endeavor known as the Angel News Network and others are also dedicated to the advancement of your species and world.

There are individuals, corporations, and governments who have hijacked our technological gifts for their own greed, profit, and gain. Each complex step in technology is another profit center for them. Even your privacy is ever being invaded. As with many natural resources (air, water, oil, gas, minerals, etc.), including cyberspace, on your planet, they are continuing to attempt to own and control what they did not create. **Dear ones, humanity cannot control nor own what it does not create**. When will you master this cosmic truth? We of Uriel are in service to the forces that created you, and maintain and sustain everything within and upon your world.

As with most of your *natural resources*, many are abusing your planet and yourselves; what was intended to be respected in balance, and freely released throughout your 3-D world, is now worldwide creating separation, lack, limitation, and addiction. Dear ones, *there is a karmic consequence for such behavior*. The universe knows quite well how to clear and cleanse itself.

Much of youth is forgoing their ability to emotionally connect, communicate, and are creating a true lack of intimacy through their addiction and misuse of the gifts of which we speak. Comfort zones and "addiction frequencies" are attaching to the individual, not unlike drug, alcohol, and sexual addictions. Our gift has become a vehicle for governments and corporations to spy upon the very people who support them. Each technical advancement appears to be an opportunity for more profit for the few from the many. Let the communication gift we have given you continue to reveal the truth, and find ways within yourselves to stop supporting the deceit and denial of the deceit.

Dear ones, these intuitive *technological* (the true IT) gifts are merely a way of showing you how **to becoming telepathic, which is your divine destiny**. It is your destiny to become directly connected to one another and Source, at no expense.

Freely mastering cyberspace through mastering yourselves is your first step to telepathy. See the loving support structures such as the Life Mastery teachings from our beloved Archangel Michael as a vital tool in freeing you from you.

Wake up and take your self-empowerment back, and apply the new technologies to truly support your higher selves and good. Allow these advancements to be a way to free yourself from the dense human structure that has imprisoned you far too long, rather than allowing it to imprison you further!

Each of you is a unique expression of the Source that created and maintains and sustains you. Your talents and gifts are vital to the process of which we speak. The technology that we gift you is the means and ways for you to serve yourself and your world.

Please remember, dear ones, when civilizations like Atlantis decided they could use our gifts not for the good of all and disregarded the consequences, they no longer existed. As soon as humanity shows it is ready for more advanced knowledge, it shall be forthcoming, and it will amaze and delight you. But right now it appears many cosmic secrets are best kept secret.

Dear ones, this particular energy/consciousness of archangelic frequency assists humanity in your relationship with your emotional and mental bodies, in order to better distribute the power of cosmic universal flow. Again, there are many tools available to support you in this truth. When the student is ready, the teacher appears.

As other higher realms have taught you, we are also asking that you examine your emotions and thoughts that create your reality. In this particular teaching, we are referring to your relationship with our gifts of technology and your self-empowerment to use them for the highest good of humanity, not someone's bank account. Remember, the natural resources on your planet belong to the forces that created them. It is a privilege for you to use them in balance, not own nor control them. When you are ready to honor and reconnect with the Source that created ALL THERE IS, you will be ready for your final golden age.

Beloveds, it is your destiny to master self and the universe/multiverse alike. Know and honor this truth, and the mysteries of creation are yours.

MERKABA

The merkaba is the way
To wed the spirit
To the body
So they don't oddly separate.

Everything in the universe
Has a merkaba,
In order to be unified and
Make-able and not break-able.

"Mer" means vehicle
In order to cycle things about.

"Ka" means light
So that things stay bright and right.

"Ba" means body
So we have something to contain,
And maintain and sustain it all.

Blessed is the marvelous, macambo merkaba,
For dancing all about,
And making all things amazingly plausible.

CHAPTER 35

THE HUMAN CONTRACT

From the Archangelic Realm of Uriel

Dear Beloved Human Sisters and Brothers,
    As an essential aspect of your awakening, it is time for you to know more deeply who you are and what being human really means, dear ones.

Prior to incarnating into human form, you agreed to become human and to experience all that you have experienced through your many lifetimes on this planet. What exactly does this mean? It means through your emotional, mental, and physical bodies you would experience every aspect of these bodies as learning tools. And through taking ownership of this truth, you will ultimately free yourself from these bodies and the bonds that have kept you within the frequency of existence you are in now.

Why would you choose such a thing? Because you are preparing yourselves to become the master teachers of this planet in world service (we consciousness)

and to evolve further out into galactic and universal service to ALL THERE IS.

As many of you know, your often not-so-loved planet has chosen to activate her soul plan to return to light (the destiny of all dense bodies, including you). Thus, all things within and upon the planet will transmute back into light, as well. *We all ultimately return to the components of our creation: light and love.* **This is the cycle of creation, dear ones.**

The missing wisdom in most human thinking is the reality that you have had the many lifetimes you have had on this planet, experiencing all you agreed to experience to learn what you needed to learn to complete your soul plans. This has prevented knowledge from becoming conscious wisdom. This veil of not knowing, remembering and knowing in the present is being lifted at this time (as part of your ascension process).

The reason it existed was for you to fully experience the now. Now that you are entering your final two-thousand-year cycle of ascension on this planet, you are fully awakening to that we speak of now.

Through your many past and present lifetimes, you have experienced every aspect of humanity possible. You have been saints and murderers; you have been killed and killed others; you have been male and female, all races, all sexual preferences, and all religions. You have embraced all belief systems, which have not always contained truth. Dear ones, you have been everything there is to be as a human. And why? To know *what is* through *what is not* is a most powerful learning experience, indeed! After all, it's how you and your soul chose the way you needed to learn what you fully needed to learn to become these master teachers of the world and beyond. **This is who you are and why you have been dancing the cosmic choreography, dear ones!**

It is time to connect the macrocosm with the microcosm, dear ones. To know the truth of what your being here really means for yourselves, one another, this world, and worlds beyond.

You have agreed to be and experience all that you have throughout your Earth time not as a punishment but as a preparation for your divine destiny to enter first into world service of oneness (we consciousness) and then beyond.

There is much to be self-mastered within the here and now prior to evolving further into your service to ALL THERE IS. From higher realms, such as we of Uriel and many others, you are receiving teachings and tools beyond the human mind to free you from your human minds and emotions that have kept you in lack and limitation. **This is the mission of the endeavor you call the Angel News Network.**

As you further awaken, you are expressing your fatigue with being in lack and limitation, the few controlling the many, your weariness with the deceit and denial of the deceit in your world. Your souls are demanding and commanding you to know who you truly are and why you are here: to now create a world of equality, harmony, and balance.

Each of you is a unique expression of creation through your divine soul plans, your talents and gifts. Your truth, needs, and boundaries are the same, dear ones. You are all created through the same energy building blocks of love: to be love and to be loved, and to love one another.

You are beginning to learn what love really is, and that, being human, you have not always understood or expressed divine true love. Love is not the emotion or feeling you think it is. It is a higher aspect of yourself that is the pathway to awakening you into your ascended mastership of self. A process of inside out (not outside in) that will allow love to be the energy/ force to create a world that knows you are all built upon this energy: **that you are one energy construction**. That each atom and electron within your being is constructed of love, and is intended to be nothing but love/loving—in spite of how humanity has distorted love/loving.

The organ that is constructed of love is your heart, dear ones. Its DNA contains all the wisdom from past and present lives, and you are now learning *to think* with your hearts, to truly access love and express it within the relationship with self, thus others. As has been said, the mind, housed within your mental body, is lovingly moving back into service to the heart. The necessary mind is not to be eliminated but curtailed in its asserted force of action (the masculine energy). As you examine your history, you can easily see where your mind, leading the way, has gotten humanity. Now, through a balance of the masculine mind and feminine heart energies (and this has nothing to do with your genders, dear ones), you are creating a pathway to freedom and oneness, which can be expanded beyond your world.

Again, let us remind you that this is happening now due to the dispensation of ascension and your destiny as being human. The contract that you agreed upon to become human contained a time line that you are completing now. It is not the end of the world, but the end of the world you have known in the past and present. If the world you have had in the past and present continued, you would destroy yourself. You have done this before. But your home and planet has made another choice. Remember, it is the love of the Source that created you, the destiny of your planet and you upon her that is creating the ascension into higher consciousness.

It is the intention of the realm of Uriel that you know these truths and apply them into your current thinking and feelings; thoughts and emotions that greatly affect you, all the elements of your world, and the universe.

HOW WE ARE MADE

Our individuated self
Often "thinks" that
Its energy and power
Exists from itself.
Forgetting every aspect of self
Came from the God-Self.

Our mental body forgot
Even the atoms from our physical bodies
Are loaned by a force outside self.
Funny how the mind wants to take credit all the time.

Let us fill our hearts with gratitude
For the multitudes

Of everything given to us
From higher altitudes.

For in truth, every aspect of self
Is borrowed from the shelf
Of the Great Chef
Who mixed and made self.

CHAPTER 36

THE MAGICAL MAGNETIC GRID

Earth Teachings from Archangel Uriel

Dear Magical Human Beings,

Your sciences are finally able to begin to understand the magical energetic components of your planet. There are unseen forces that prevent your daily destruction that also promise to become free energy sources for all, and much more.

There is an energy grid inside the core of your planet that works together with physical crystalline structures (crystals) and portals/vortices on the surface of the planet on which you humans reside. Humanity is in the process of transmuting from a dense carbon-based structure to a lighter, higher-vibrational crystalline structure (our ascension process). The totality of this energy grid affects all things inside and upon the body of the planet. The energies from this grid go out from within and form an etheric grid around the entire planet, not only protecting the planet, but affecting your human emotional, mental, and physical bodies, as well. **Human consciousness is also**

rising as the planet's energy increases. So, in effect, Mother Earth is birthing the new you.

As an essential aspect of your divine destiny, this grid continues to receive upgrades, shifting us from one epoch to another—most recently, Piscean (masculine) to Aquarian (feminine) energies. This not so simply means that both **assertive masculine and receptive feminine energies are moving into balance**. Your evolutionary path cannot go forward without this occurrence. You are currently experiencing the imbalance of these two vital energies; a lack of equality, harmony, and balance.

The founders of the Angel News Network were led to the major energetic vortex/portal of Mount Shasta to serve as proxies for humanity and assist in the advancement of energetic balances for the entire planet.

This was achieved through two sacred journeys there in 2010 and 2011. From Mount Shasta (in Northern California), all energies are initially showered onto the planet from the galactic core and the Milky Way that hit the planetary grid, the main and first entry point for the planet. From these points, the energies are distributed throughout the planetary grid worldwide.

This energetic grid is integrated through sacred geometrics into your individuated soul plans, and then your emotional, mental, and physical bodies, allowing how you feel and think to manifest a higher consciousness to activate your purpose in being here (to learn to love).

In the beginning of New Age thinking, it was believed that a global shift (ascension) would take place through a series of infusions of energy to the planet herself, and then from the planet to each person individually—sort of an automatic process. Many thought 2012 was that moment. In reality, what needs to happen is each of us, *as cells of the body of the planet*, must **anchor and integrate these energetic frequencies individually** to fully account for all the unique configurations of human consciousness (each unique soul plan).

Another way to explain this ascension process is to say your unique individual soul plan crystalline grid (the DNA matrix) will shift in a slightly different manner for each of you, since you are all unique divine expressions of God experiencing itself. In being and doing this, you will maintain and sustain the full spectrum of vibrations needed for a true global shift. Now you can better see the interrelationship of your planet and yourselves.

As equal and balanced energies harmonize for larger and larger communities of individuals (who accomplish their individual shifts), the global shift will manifest in ever-increasing frequencies, creating a quantum effect. As the planet's magnetic grid shifts, the surface crystal grids will be reborn. This process is happening now.

The next meaningful grid shift is that of human consciousness. There is much planetary and personal clearing and cleansing taking place now in terms of energies being received and consciousness rising.

It is important to see communities of equality, harmony, and balance being created, and their intention to fully support the Earth and all within and upon her body.

WHAT ARE THE EFFECTS AND USES OF THE ENHANCED PLANETARY CRYSTAL GRID AT THIS TIME?

The crystal grid, or sometimes called the crystal life stream, has basically two aspects; one is **physical** and the other **etheric**. This is the composition of most things within the universe, including you. **The primary reasons for the grid are for energy amplification in the physical and storage and transfer of information in the etheric.**

The grid is a direct conduit for human consciousness to access and bring joyful perception into the denser Earth frequency (3-D). It is the 3-D that is being elevated/raised during what we call the ascension process (our divine destiny at this time line now). As you might imagine, the crystal grid has always been in place within and around the planet. *What you are experiencing now is an expansion of the effects of the grid in the planet and human DNA.* This is a direct result of the ascension of the energies of the crystal grid into higher and purer vibrations.

What you are experiencing now, as you interact with the crystal grid in the ascension process, is what the planet herself chose to undergo as an essential part of her soul plan. Through this integration/interaction with the planet's process, your physical bodies are also restructuring (moving from a dense carbon to a lighter crystalline structure). **Your crystalline structure is ascending through the adjustment of your DNA, day by day, through the energies of your**

heart. This happens as you increase and maintain your level/quota of love and light, day by day, moment by moment. This is the way you have chosen to learn. *What is actually happening is that your believing mind is moving back into service to the knowing and loving heart.*

WHY IS THIS HAPPENING?

Your planet goes through major cosmic cycles of twenty-six thousand years and smaller two-thousand-year cycles within the twenty-six thousand.

Your Earth is now within one of the major cycles of moving into a higher level of existence, thus everything within and upon her body will move also, including humanity. **Each one of you has also chosen a new life without duality and death through your soul plan's activation.**

Endeavors such as the Angel News Network and many others are connecting with the higher-realm frequencies to bring their tools and teachings to assist you. The vibrational shift of the grid is taking place whether you are aware of it or not. Each of your vibrational frequencies is also entraining itself to that of the grid. **Thus, the entire planet is now fully involved in the ascension process**.

As light workers and way showers, it is helpful to interact with the grid in a more conscious way in order to gain a fuller understanding of its uses. If it resonates, make a commitment within your heart space to access the grid for the good of all. During past golden ages such as Atlantis, the grid was often accessed for corrupt purposes. While the past lessons learned were essential, humankind still has a way to go.

The archangel realms, such as we of Uriel, were instrumental in the gifting of your present cyberspace

technologies in order to assist in freeing yourselves from 3-D controls. Much of the present abuse and addictive use of these technologies is similar to past advanced ages. Know that the extreme misuse/abuse or intention to harm others will not be allowed to happen again. Those who continue to attempt harm will experience a swift return of their energies inverted upon themselves and the karmic consequences of any harmful agenda.

Due to past abuses, from many epochs since the fall of both Atlantis and Lemuria, the etheric crystal grid was moved farther away from the atmosphere of the planet. This decision was made by the Intergalactic Federation and Source to protect the grid from further misuse and corruption of its matrix. The planet and humanity were allowed to live without its direct influence for a very long time. **And this has dumb downed and diminished your innate spiritual abilities.** You are now in the process of reclaiming your full potential, but you have a long way to go.

With your freedom of will and choice (that no one can take away from you), you find your world poised once again at self-destruction, but not as powerful as the advanced civilizations of the past. Today, the scenario resembles more of a slow and painful autoimmune disease where the organism eats away at itself, such as cancer and HIV/AIDS, two of the largest world killers.

As the mind moves back into service to the knowing heart, **your hearts are reawakening.** You are remembering the lessons from the disconnection from Source and abuses of the past. You are ready to make a new choice and create a new world of equality, harmony, and balance.

You cannot create in the physical world without the physical process of crystallization. **Crystals, and the process through which a physical crystal is formed, unite the higher and lower aspects of the Divine, male and female, and all the elements of the Earth.**

As the etheric crystal grid once again is allowed to move closer to the service of the planet, it awakens and reunites all the energies that reside in physical crystal format. **Once again, the physical crystal grid of the planet is being reactivated with the will of the Divine.**

The full ascension process of the Earth is taking place now through this physical grid, and will continue until the vibration of the planet reaches a dimensional shift and reunites with her divine soul plan, **then human consciousness will reach a new and greater level of consciousness and a new existence.**

Through the grid, you reach into the hearts and minds of all who resonate/connect to it. You receive answers to questions asked, and the healing and manifestation energies necessary for any endeavor or service you may intend. You move from me consciousness to we consciousness, connected to higher realms and your soul plans.

The highest good use of the grid is mandatory. The higher realms are here to work with each of you in appropriate ways. Call upon them.

As many of you know, each of you is now experiencing the restructuring of your carbon-based DNA into a purer crystalline form. As a result, you are experiencing emotional, mental, and physical realignments. **These clearings and cleansings** can be painful and uncomfortable at times; this is your resistance to the shift. Become aware that all the shifts are for your highest good, and remove as much of your resistance as possible, accepting with compassion and thus forgiving how you are choosing to learn and grow.

IN CONCLUSION

Now you know more about crystals and the crystal grid. Interact with crystals in healing your past traumas and present toxic energies. Crystals are conscious beings here to support you. Connect with the crystal grid and ask for messages. Share what you receive with others in communities of equality, harmony, and balance—each of you holds a unique piece of awareness.

A MAGIC CHAIR

Legend tells of a magic chair,
Out there that can transport
Us from here to there, everywhere.

It's a magic chair
That soon will come from there
To here to move us through air and everywhere
To an amazing new way of being and seeing.

The Magical Magnetic Grid

It will assist in rising
Physical form components into
Its divine purity and structure, raising
The electronic body into bliss,
By seating and going through the mist.

Here's the reveal, once perfected,
The perfect body remains
Forever eternal youthful,
Beautiful and strong.
Wouldn't you like to have this deal,
And not have it go wrong.

In this new body
You can do anything
Wherever you choose in the universe,
With no adverse reactions,
Anytime.

Then there will be no barriers of time place,
Nor space or condition of being.
In freeing self of every conceivable
Lack and limitation in any station,
Of being.

The desire for this perfection
Exists and is an innate idea
Within many civilizations.

In many legends and myths
Of almost every race and nation
There exist stories of being
Immortal perfected beings,
Always being beautiful
From ageless age to age.
Suppose we were to tell you
This is the master blueprint
Upon which humanity was imprinted,
Eons, ago.

And that this magic chair really exists,
Right now,
And will soon persist…

CHAPTER 37

THE POWER OF
NOT KNOWING

From Archangel Uriel, World Teacher and Guardian

Dear Beloved Humans,
Oh, how the human mind loves *to think* it knows. Through what you think, you think you can possibly attempt to control, or just say you know. And this knowing makes you feel safe and secure within a world of illusion. Dear ones, the only thing that holds your 3-D world of time and distance within your form of reality is that *you think it exists*. Your thoughts and emotions around those thoughts are the elements that maintain and sustain what you think is real. **For in reality, there is no time, only now, and no distance, only presence.**

We wish to now invite you into the unknown that exists in the frequency/awareness of non-time/distance. **For in what you call the void, the unknowing, the nothing, is the world of all possibilities and probabilities that frees you from the limitations of the human mind**. The human mind has been a great tool, and as it moves into service to the knowing heart, its role will be subdued but not eliminated. Now we realize this is quite a blow to the ego housed in the mind that for eons thought it was all powerful, all knowledge and wisdom. Only through knowing otherwise can you begin to realize and accept just how magnificent and powerful you are. For where there are no limitations of thought or restraint of time/distance, *in the power of the unknown*, all things are possible. With no expectations, you ride **upon the frequency of cosmic limitless opportunities.**

The human mind has been a receiver, not an originator, of the unknowing reality assisting in moving humanity forward. It is time to really know you have been loved and supported by forces beyond your comprehension for eons, *supporting your ascension journey* into the unified world of which we speak. Once in your real reality, there is no going back.

The unknowing world offers a comprehension of a new reality that has always existed. Through this new world, you can truly set yourself **free of a world that your wounds and defenses created**. We realize this may bring up fear in some and excitement in others. *It is time to surrender to your divinity and trust and not know in order to truly know, maybe for the first time.*

Through your ascension journey of moving into a higher frequency of existence, the unseen mysteries of eternal reality are to be revealed. You will learn all that exists comes from what you call the unknowing, which is a cosmic consciousness garnered through ALL THERE IS, which has to know nothing.

You will come to know that not knowing is only not knowing when it is unknown to humanity. You will learn in the **unknowing wisdom**

truth is revealed. A truth that has the power to set you free, a freedom that becomes a universal ticket to limitless cosmic travel that you will need as master teachers of the universe.

Your religions say, "In the beginning there was the void of nothingness, and into the nothingness came a purposeful thought that filled the all-pervasive void." All that you thought created you is now moving into and beyond all that you thought. **The unknowing, the void, is not in motion, but you move through the void as your consciousness moves from one event to another. In knowing you are separate, you create duality and confrontation; in not knowing, you are all One.**

If this confuses you, turn inward to your loving heart that knows this awakened reality cannot exist without your heart, for the light of the heart always exists. Your heart knows that even infinity is moving on (as you are) to some *unthinkable* destination. Your heart knows why much of this has been hidden from humanity, waiting for your consciousness to open and receive the light. It is time to understand that humanity is of light and light is of humanity. Dear ones, know that the void, the unknowing, is filled with worlds within worlds, one within the other, separate yet one.

All that you have experienced within the knowing is to prepare you for not knowing, in order to surrender to being in service to ALL THERE IS, as the master teachers of the universe. This is the meaning, value, and purpose of your journey.

Humanity has been only what it thinks it knows. It is time to break the bondage of knowledge, being ruled by fear and control, and move into the wisdom of not knowing; to now walk down your divine

pathway of surrendering to not knowing in order to become one with all. This is how the universe works. What a mighty unknowing that created it all!

BEING PHYSICAL

In order to be fully physically formed,
We chose, it was required,
That we forget our
True Divine Essence and heritage,
So we could completely experience
All the 3D heredity.

This way we could learn
All there is to know
About what is,
Through what is not.

This lesson of learning,
Is complete,
And no longer has any yearning.

It is now time to command and demand,
That this forgetting veil
Be sent to jail,
And never seen again.

CHAPTER 38

A DIVINE DESTINATION: YOUR DIVINITY

From the Great White Brotherhood

Dear Sisters and Brothers,
    All of your lifetimes lead to the same destination (how and when you get there are your choices): the eternal connection to your divinity. *You need not believe this; it does not matter.* For you will come to this truth on your own when you are ready, through your freedom of will and choice.

You will reach your divine destination when you have learned all you need to learn by not knowing it. One of your favorite learning tools is learning "what is" through "what is not." You have eons of examples of this. There are easier ways to learn, but this seems to be the one most of you prefer and need.

Your judgment, shaming, blaming, duality, separation, and confrontation are some of your favorite dense-frequency tools to the divine destination of which we speak. Dear ones, there is no right or wrong, or good or bad, to the process: it simply "is." These are all aspects of the same thing. Darkness allows you to know there is light.

When you reach your divine destination (your direct connection to ALL THERE IS), only you need to know and accept and welcome your arrival.

Dear ones, all your lives on this planet have been a *constant beginning, not an end.* Your extended purpose in being will grow and expand when you set yourself free from the dense frequency where you currently reside to become the master teachers of the universe. (The reason you signed on to all this!) The most essential tools in gaining your freedom are your resonance and discernment. These will show you your UNIQUE PATH to your destination of divinity.

As you have heard many times before, the universe would be incomplete without each and every one of you (this includes the minerals, plants, and animals, as well). Can you receive this truth now? Take a deep breath and receive some more of this truth now.

None of your journey is about real or unreal, seen or unseen, or knowledge; *it is about truth and wisdom (collected over many lifetimes).* **Wisdom is truth reflecting the Cosmic Law of Love—that being you and God Power.**

Love and truth are inseparable, eternal, and unchanging. These can be known but not changed. Love and truth are the essential aspects of ALL THERE IS; they are beyond teaching and time. They can be best found within and through a personal process examination of yourself. (See Life Mastery, www.theangelnewsnetwork.com.)

Dear ones, your journey has no beginning, it has no end. IT SIMPLY IS a choice you made in agreeing to be human, experiencing all aspects of humanity being God. In reality, none of your 3-D life path can exist apart from the higher realms from whence it originated.

Your 3-D world is composed of beliefs in opposites and separate wills, often leading to confrontation. Look at your world right now. **This world leads to constant resistance since it is not really who you are.**

The good news is that you are in the process of waking up and knowing your life and world have been illusions you created in order to learn from it and to leave it. It's all been a "Lover-versity." **The world you have created is merely a reflection of your internal relationship with yourself based upon a lack of love.** Since love is the building block of ALL THERE IS, and ALL THERE IS is all there is, it can ask for nothing else.

As you continue to wake up from your 3-D illusion by accepting with compassion and forgiving why you created it all, you can choose **forgiveness**. Through forgiveness you can remember who you are and why you are here by releasing/graduating yourself from the **cosmic classroom you created** to now know the truth.

You are God experiencing itself in all ways in order to master density and to release yourself from it, in order to enter and be in service to ALL THERE IS. Remember always, this will **allow you to become the master teachers of the universe, your purpose in being here.**

Now you are remembering, for what we have just said is all stored in your heart. Access your heart, dear ones, when you forget again. It is all eternally stored there.

THE WONDERFUL WHEEL

There is a Wonderful Wheel of wonderment
Which affects the welfare of the whole world.

It activates the direction of Light,
Within the sustained systems to which
We exit and persist.

When that wheel wanders into
The Way of Humanity,
And is nearer than we are aware of,
The wheel releases rays of light,
Upon the world,
And all our resistance to the light
Clears in sheer delight.

When we become spokes on
That great wheel,
That radiate out,
It creates a rotation,
That will allow no doubt.
Then we remember we are the Light.

CHAPTER 39

WHETHER THE WEATHER

From the Archangelic Realm of Uriel

Dear Beloved Weathered Humans,

We come to you at this time with a brief reminder and essential message about your growth and expansion into who you truly are and why you are here (to be in world service to one another and the forces that created you). **Dear ones, your emotions and thoughts create all weather patterns upon your planet**. Pay attention to **where and when weather conditions appear** throughout your world. Yes, you have seasonal patterns, but there are also "events" within your seasons that are representative of the necessary clearing and cleansing of your Mother Earth from your abuse of her body. **You simply will not be allowed to continue this abuse and survive**.

Your planet has activated an ascension process, and those upon her conscious body that know and understand the abuse needs to stop are welcome to join the journey. (Creating free, non-planet-based energy sources will also soon further assist you; more on this later.)

We of the frequency and consciousness of Uriel are involved in all the elements that affect your world, dear ones. The ones that appear to be most hidden from humanity relate to how your emotions, and thoughts, thus actions, affect your planet, your home. If it resonates, pay attention to where what you call "acts of God" (acts of humanity), and what you call extreme or unusual weather, take place, and the emotional and mental environments of the people in those geographical locations.

Dear ones, your emotions and thoughts collect and accumulate within your atmosphere, and when they reach a crucial mass there is a release, in order to clear and cleans those emotions and thoughts from the planet. In many ways, you are just beginning to understand the cosmic truth of which we speak; thus, further knowing how powerful you are and how that power affects you and your world.

The weather is one of the essential ways your conscious planet, a living being, can survive the unconscious behavior of those humans upon her body.

Look at where storms such as your hurricanes and earthquakes originate, their travel paths and where they land. Pay attention to the human emotional and mental conditions in these geographical locations, and what type of negative human actions take place there.

Within advanced 5-D civilizations the weather is perfect each day, due to the ability of the inhabitants to monitor their emotions and thoughts, thus respecting self, one another, and their planet.

Dear ones, if you choose not to wake up, the weather conditions on your planet can become more severe. If you choose not to understand the cause and effect of your world, the planet knows exactly how to balance herself. Remember, dear ones, you are dealing with forces that created you and are much more powerful and loving than you at present. **You are in service to those forces, not they to you**. In your past and present, you have attempted to control "nature" and bend her to your will. This short-term goal has not served your highest good or that of your planet. It is time to make another choice, if you so choose. (Not understanding this truth was the demise of all past golden ages.)

Once you fully wake up and realize you are in world service to one another and ALL THERE IS, your lives can become filled with grace, ease, and perfect weather. **Think of the loss that your bad weather costs you, dear ones.**

If you so choose, it is time to begin to understand the relationship of your emotions and thoughts, and how they affect yourselves and your world, in order to create a more perfect world, and a final golden age of equality, harmony, and balance for all.

THE SUN

The Sun of our Solar System
Is to the whole universal system
What our heart is to the human body.

The sun's rays of energy
Are the blood-stream system
Of this world, and beyond, it seems.

The lungs of Earth
Is the girth of the atmosphere,
Surrounding the planet,
Through which the effects of Sun's energy,
Constantly flow,
Clearing and cleansing the Earth,
As they go.

In addition to our heart,
The Sun is also our head,
The Father of the Family, if you will,
Of this entire family system,
Conducting the eternal energy,
Through freedom of will.

Want a shock; the sun is not hot,
As we think.
It's cool as a summer cucumber,
Gentle as an afternoon slumber.
It only needs to get hot,
When it passes through the gases
And near Earth's atmosphere.

Then Sun's energy becomes the electronic
Hold and pole of the Earth's magnetic poles,

And then the Mind of God,
Unites with the Soul of the Earth.
This is why we are the Suns/Sons of God,
Similar to the Sun,
Being one.

CHAPTER 40

THREE GROUPS OF PEOPLE

From Archangel Uriel, World Teacher and Guardian

Dear Beloved Children of Our Divine Earth,
    How many of you are feeling loved and divine at this moment? As we once again focus on the intentions and purposes of people, we would like to share the following observation: there are three basic groups of people in your world at the moment. These groups are creating the world that you are currently experiencing.

(1) There are those of you who manifest and create *newness in the world*, serving the good of all. In your vernacular, "they make things happen." They see themselves worthy enough to be who they are, knowing who they are and why they are here.

(2) There are those of you who *simply watch* what is happening, and who often judge it as a reflection of your relationship with self, not seeing self as good enough. There is no positive feeling into action.

(3) There are those of you who are **blind to what is happening**, indifferent, and hold on to the old, literally for dear life, with a deep fear of change or surrendering to not knowing.

Which are you, dear ones? People of numbers two and three often shame, blame, and judge those of number one, and, **ironically, open themselves to be controlled by others**. The peoples of number one are given the opportunity to choose to create a new paradigm of equality, harmony, and balance. **These three groups have kept humanity in a push-and-pull cycle for eons. That is about to shift.**

You each have a *divine soul plan* containing your purpose and reason to be here. What is yours, dear ones? At this time, take a deep breath and connect with your heart; connect with your *talents and gifts* that can and will be a *direct expression of your divinity and love of self*, and *allow access to your soul plan*.

Ask yourself, "Who am I? Why am I here?" Once you know the "who" and the "why," the rest will appear/build with grace and ease. This awareness, this wisdom, will transform/transmute you into people number one (if you are not already there), and allow you to further heal self and move your weary world into communities of love and divinity.

THESE THREE

From many ancient texts, sent asunder:

(1) The most powerful and loving
Force is that which created us.
The greatest happiness
Comes from adoring and exploring
Your Source of ALL.

(2) The most eternal and real
Force is the I AM PRESENCE
Within each of us.
Stand true to the I AM
Within you.

(3) The most truthful force
Is The Light, as us.
Allow your Light
To eliminate your shadow
In the bright.

So be these three...

CHAPTER 41

UNIVERSAL LAW OF CAUSE AND EFFECT

From Archangel Uriel, World Teacher and Guardian

Dear Beloved Humans, meaning "God being man,"
There are universal laws throughout the universe that allow creation to be, and to remain in balance. One of these laws is called CAUSE AND EFFECT. It is time to know such laws exist and learn how to apply them, if you so choose.

The Law states: THERE IS ALWAYS A REASON (CAUSE) TO ANY RESULT (EFFECT).

Humanity often has not been aware of this law or has chosen to ignore it, with dire consequences. We are once again asking you *to connect the causes and effects in your life in order to create the life you say you want.*

Your not being able to connect *cause and effect* has created much imbalance and unnecessary suffering in your lives and world. By becoming conscious of how *cause and effect* works and becoming accepting and compassionate about it, you can greatly alter/affect what is transpiring in your life and world.

In effect, you are the Creators of the world around you. The aim is to take OWNERSHIP of this moment by moment; to know that what affects one, affects all.

Dear ones, all causes bring forth effects, and vice versa. Your present and future varies as cause brings forth effect. By looking deeply into the cause, you will see that all is affected.

All cause and effect are affected by your freedom of choice and will; look within the causation and you will find the effect. By becoming better aware of the effect that follows the cause, you can create a higher-frequency effect, if you so choose.

The soul journey of humanity has often been filled with struggle as a result of a lack of awareness and compassion for *cause and effect. If you so choose, you can begin to make new choices as you see the effect of cause and effect within your ascension process.*

Know, dear ones, you are destined to proceed ever onward, moved by the Universal Law of Cause and Effect, until in the end both become one. That is the reason the law exists; as darkness = light; problem = solution; wrong = right; giving = receiving; masculine = feminine; AS ALL BECOMES ONE.

Soon, if you so choose, you will see ALL IS ONE, including yourselves. The Law of Cause and Effect is just another way to get you to your Oneness.

Remember, dear ones, the universe is filled with laws to maintain and sustain itself, often to protect itself from unconscious/abusive behavior like yours. If you so choose, it is time to wake up, become aware of these laws, and learn how to apply them in order to create a life of grace and ease.

CAUSE AND EFFECT

There is a cosmic law
Called Cause and Effect
That automatically balances
In order to prevent a wreck.

This balancing process addresses,
And governs all forces everywhere
So we don't have to ever care.
If we understand this law,
We don't have to see human experiences
As wholly flawed.

This law is the only logical explanation
For the infinite complexities,
And experiences of many people and nations.

There really is no such thing
As chance or accident
That really never had
A true ring.

All is really under direct and,
Exact perfect law,
Where there can be no rawness.

For every experience
Has a former cosmic cause
Since everything is
The cause of a future eternal effect,
Thus, all can be correct.
Are we all set?

If you should injure one
Through one's life,
You are certain to know that form
In another life,
And endure that strife.

Through Cause and Effect
We can experience everything
Possible in the world
To know in effect
We are the same persona and thing.
Through freedom of choice and will,
We shall keep creating Cause and Effect
Till we know full well,
Our purpose is to,
Balance giving and receiving, female and male.

And then you'll really know
There is no such thing as we call
Hell.

CHAPTER 42

UNIVERSAL LAWS OF SELF-EMPOWERMENT AND LOVE

Inspired by Archangels Gabriel, Michael, Raphael, and Uriel

Greetings, Beloved Humans, being the best you can be, We come to you once again with a message and teaching of love and support for the journey you have chosen to be human on this planet Earth; a planet that has been "seeded" by twelve different star systems in order to create a diversity of a LOVER-VERSITY like no other in the universe. For you are **simply here to learn how to love** self, first and foremost, in order to love one another and create the world of Oneness you are destined to create. The twelve Universal Laws we are now to share once again are to honor and support your highest good and a way to free yourselves from yourselves, if you so choose.

The basis of all your duality, separation, and often confrontation is the result of your relationship with

yourself. You have heard many times *the only relationship you are having is the one with yourself. The taught shame of self is the reason for every emotional, mental, and physical imbalance (dis-ease). Let you now reprogram yourselves and create a new reality through a loving relationship with self, by better* **understanding what has caused your lack of self-love, and how to move through the lack to love.**

While each of the following twelve laws represent gifts from the various worlds that help create and maintain and sustain you, **each** *law builds upon the other, no matter what order they are in. Are you ready to create a new, loving you?*

SELF-ACCEPTANCE

Can you accept with compassion, thus forgive, all the ways you have chosen to learn what you came here to learn? Taking **ownership** of your choices is vital. It is time to release all shaming, blaming, and judgment of self that allows that of others. You cannot shame, blame, nor judge another without first doing the same to yourself. Rather than focusing on what is not in your life, focus on what is. Make a list of your assets and liabilities, and see what you would like to maintain and sustain in your life.

SELF-KNOWLEDGE

Two of the most important phrases ever created are KNOW THYSELF and TO THINE OWN SELF BE TRUE. It is essential to know WHO YOU ARE and WHY YOU ARE HERE. **What is your purpose in being here?** What are your talents and gifts you uniquely wish to bring into world service? Create a divine soul plan for yourself. You can begin by listing your qualities, talents, and abilities. The Angel News Network has many teachings to assist you in better knowing yourself. **Once you firmly know who you are and why you are here, you can build the what, where, when, and how of your life.**

SELF-WORTH

A basis for many human lacks is not feeling good enough or worthy enough to embrace all the abundance of life. You are not born feeling not good enough or worthy enough. People who profess to love you but do not fully love themselves teach you this. As a result, you create self-imposed limitations and lacks that you can now release by becoming conscious of them. List where you feel deprived and make another choice to receive.

SELF-ESTEEM

Your self-esteem is your view of and feeling about yourself. How do you see yourself right now? Stand in front of a mirror unclothed and see what feelings and judgment come up about yourself. From whence did this chatter come? It came from your **sabotaging mental body that was taught by others**. This is not the truth. You are a divine being having a human experience just the way you have chosen. It is time, if you so choose, to see your goodness. Look in that mirror and praise yourself; begin a "good book," listing all the little and not-so-little good things you do for yourself and others each day.

SELF-CONFIDENCE

Self-confidence is the wisdom of knowing you are capable of being and doing what is important to you. You all have moments of not being sure about this. **Surrender to not**

always knowing and allow the probabilities and possibilities of not knowing to flow through. Self-confidence is not to be confused with arrogance, which is a defense for a lack of self-confidence. Begin writing down your accomplishments; you'll be surprised and delighted with how confident you are. Remember, you are Creation/God/Source expressing itself.

SELF-RESPECT
People who have self-respect are able to speak their truth, express their needs, and set their boundaries (with no intention of harm), and allow others to do the same. Do you know your truth, needs, and boundaries? Many do not know their truth, or accept and know their needs, thus do not set any boundaries and become consumed by others through their lack of self-respect. The Angel News Network has many tools to assist you in knowing your truth, needs, and boundaries. If not now, when will you stand in your truth, needs, and boundaries with no intention to harm? **Knowing how others respond or react is their process, not your concern.**

SELF-SERVICE
Self-service means you are able to take care of your truth, needs, and boundaries by prioritizing them. At the beginning and end of each day, review what was incomplete and needs to take place the next day. Ask yourself, what do I not like to do that would serve me if these things were done?

SELF-DISCIPLINE
Self-discipline is the ability to **routinely practice** your talents, abilities, and qualities of self, which creates and

supports your self-empowerment. This may require you to move out of your comfort zones of habits and patterns that may be limiting and to support the ones that create growth and expansion.

SELF-FORGIVENESS

The components of forgiveness are acceptance and compassion. Can you accept with compassion, thus forgive, the ways you have chosen to learn what you need to learn in being human? Through your **ownership** and forgiveness you move from victimhood to self-empowerment. This will set you free from the "me."

SELF-CRITICISM

Through your resonance (internal gyro system) and discernment you can look at your limitations without shaming, blaming, or judging them. You can look at what you want and need, and see what stands in the way of that and ways to improve yourself. **All mistakes are simply a way to learn**, not to punish you. Every problem is the other side of the solution. All this is an essential part of the choice you made to be human and experience this frequency.

SELF-IMPROVEMENT

The purpose of life is growth and expansion; this includes you, your planet, solar system, galaxy, universe, and multiverse. It's not a matter of being better than someone else; it's being who you came here to be, letting go of being special in order to embrace the ordinariness of being fully human, which is divine.

SELF-RELIANCE

Once you remember and know your are God/Creation/Source experiencing itself, you can embrace the reality that you have fragments within your soul plan that ensure your self-reliance through your talents and gifts. You do not have to be dependent on anyone else for the reality of who you are. Are you ready to receive this? If not, there are many endeavors here to support you in this truth. This is one of many!

IN CONCLUSION

To reiterate, this is one of many endeavors/teachings to allow you to know and embrace the truth of who you are and why you are here. You are never alone. You are loved and supported by forces beyond your comprehension that will love you unconditionally until you do yourself.

THE POWER WITHIN

Throughout humanity's history
People have not understood
Life,
Thus, much strife has withstood.
People seem to drop into depression
Rather than understand how life
Can compress into compassion.

They seem not to know
Their blessings are the result
Of something within,
Rather than outside in.

It is an innate fantastic force
That's always been there.
It's just a matter of accepting it,
And bringing it to the fore.

All that we've experienced
Is meant to awaken this internal force,
And know we are the source within.

Through this Self-Source
We can know who we are,
And why we are here,
And then the real fun can begin.

Once we know the Source
We can choose to be in service to All,
And never have to fall, again.

Then forever more...
It's win, win, win, win, win.

CHAPTER 43

YOU AND YOUR PLANET'S PURPOSE

From Archangel Uriel, World Teacher and Guardian

Dear Beloved Earth Beings,

Greetings, Beloved Beings of Earth, as we of the consciousness and Archangelic Realm of Uriel come to you at this most important time in your planet's history and mission for existing. Do you know your planet's reasons to be or your purpose in being here, dear ones? The truth of these has been veiled for you far too long, and the time to know the truth and "BE" able to do something about this has come.

Your planet and your species are at a crossroads of no return. You cannot return to your past and present ways of behavior and survive as a species and planet. Many teachings and tools outside the human mind have been coming to you to assist you in escaping yourselves. The human mind alone is composed of wounded elements (altered egos) that often prevent you from succeeding and revealing your true higher selves and nature. These are elements within your mind through your freedom of choice and will that have not served you well. You have been gifted with this freedom of will and choice, which you have chosen to move you as far from your truth and purpose as possible. You are on the brink of annihilation.

Why do we of the Archangelic Realm of Uriel come to you, dear ones? As your mission is to learn to love one another (that includes your planet home), our mission in service to the God-consciousness, Source, ALL THERE IS—whatever you choose to call the forces of creation—is to assist and support you in your mission. Each of the archangelic realms has a priority, if you will. We were keenly involved in the origin and creation of your planet, as well as maintaining and sustaining you both now.

So maybe the best way to explain our purpose in coming to you now is to explain your origin and remind you of your reason to be here.

As many of you know, none of you originated from this planet. Your history books and explanation of the evolution of mankind are nowhere near true. They express a small fraction of your beginnings and express nothing of your reason to be.

Long, long, long ago in your human time, where there is no time, you were conceived within a glorious concept and mission of a world that would be created of the most magnificent components of the multiverse (all the universes combined). A world that would represent the most diverse aspects of creation—a divine experiment that, if it succeeded, would alter creation forever. In order to achieve this, it meant many forces of creation had to come together and offer the most glorious aspects of himself or herself to this mission. Thus, councils from twelve star systems met through the Intergalactic Federation to create such a wondrous world. Each star system offered the highest expression of itself to the effort. This was infused within a DNA energetic format readied to combine with the others, thus creating a unique blueprint for a new marvelous world we call Earth.

QUEST FOR TRUTH

We are beginning to remember
Our Oneness with ALL THERE IS.
Life is a journey about self-empowerment and realization,
Filled with our chosen teachings' revelations.

The bonds of untruth remain strong,
As we seek to eliminate the wrong.

Let us never abandon the quest for the truth,
For the truth will set us free
From you and from me.

Real truth, new truth is
Being revealed now.
If they resonate, apply them,
If not, deny them.
The new truths are waiting

Those who can accept them,
And let the old beliefs
Die like a whim in the wind.

CHAPTER 44

ACCEPTING CHANNELING URIEL

From Archangel Uriel, World Teacher and Guardian

Dear Divine Channel,

Oh, happy days! We are delighted with your choice to work with us, dear one. Welcome. There is much work to be done at this most dramatic time of change upon your planet. Much is being revealed to humanity of the many levels of assistance you are receiving, if you choose it. There has never been in the history of your planet such a "concert" of effort from the angelic and star realms. But remember, dear ones, we can only do so much. You have freedom of will and choice. We cannot and must not interfere. But forces like never before are coming into your world to assist you, at last, to join into oneness. To stop the few controlling the many, if you so choose.

Your summer will be a most powerful time. We shall see those who choose to move forward and those who do not. Those who do not will no longer receive the assistance of the past times. Our focus is upon the portion of your beautiful planet that chooses to move forward into oneness—the Club of Love, Acceptance, Peace, Unity, Oneness. How does that make you feel in contrast to your planet's past and present history of separation and war?

By the end of your hot summer months, we'll have all the forces connected to assist in allowing the greatest truth to come forth for you all: to know that you are spiritual beings having a human experience. We have watched lovingly throughout your history as you chose not to love one another, as a collective whole. Now you can see that you are all unique expressions of that whole.

There are many institutions and governments and their leaders that will facilitate this shift. Pay attention to whom you put into office, know their true intention, check their background. Reform your "professional" political career structure.

Remember, it was the private common man that was to go into public office, then return to his private life after servicing his fellow man. Not professional politicians who through generational greed have created your corrupt system. You can change that now, dear ones.

The feminine energies coming in will assist in balancing the masculine that has created much of your cause and effect. There must be a balance of male and female energies; this has nothing to do with either gender or sex. These energies are here to assure that love stays in place, for when the male and female balance, it equals love. Then you think with your hearts, which is your true mind, not your brain.

Set aside all fear and resistance as the changes take place. Remember, fear is just an absence of the love you've needed all along. And love is the glue that holds the universe together, the highest vibration that allows great, creative, loving things to manifest into your third-dimensional world.

Don't worry about how all this will happen. Surrender to the unknown. In the void lies creation and all possibility. In the not knowing, the knowing will surely come. There is no need to strive for anything. The divine plan of your planet is unfolding through your individual divine plans. It's all perfect, dear ones. Fear not, love is on the way to save the day!

Now rest and know the truth of who you are and why you are. It is all being revealed. Relax, love, rest. And listen to that quiet voice within you. It is we speaking to you, guiding many of you. Use your solitude to know the quiet and truth coming forth. You will not find it outside in your world. It lies deep with yourself. It's been there all along. Now you know for sure.

P.S. Many of you use forming groups to facilitate the work that needs to be done. State the intention/mission of the group and allow those souls who resonate within it to appear. Remember change is all there is. Allow your fellow man an opportunity to change or not. Through holding the focus/mission of your groups you will know who the light workers are. Allow all to become so. The history of your planet has excluded most by the few. Don't fall into that trap again, dear ones. The portion of your planet that is there to be and do the work will just appear. They will reveal themselves soon enough. Know this present truth and be free of your past history.

CHANNELING HIGHER REALMS

The best way to connect and channel with higher realms
Is to get yourself out of the way.
In fact, that is the only way
To receive a clear, concise message,
Not filled with your filter.

Begin by stating to yourself,
This is not about me,
I clear myself of myself,
In order to receive,
And be in service to the we.

Channeled information is best
Received by those
Who have chosen to arrest
Themselves in a personal process,
Clearing and releasing wounds,
Ego defenses, and the rest.

This allows a state of neutrality,
Moving me out of the way,
To be a good messenger
For myself and others
That day.

CHAPTER 45

COMPETITON: WINNING AND LOSING

From Archangel Uriel, World Teacher and Guardian

Dearest Beloved Human Sisters and Brothers,

Life is not about winning nor losing nor competing with one another, dear ones, especially if others are harmed emotionally, mentally, or physically. Where in your lives are you still valuing competing with one another in business, education, sports, religions, and relationships with self and others?

While you may think you have something called "team spirit" (an illusion of oneness through an aspect of the assertive masculine energy), it often creates imbalances of "not good or worthy enough," narcissism, and deceit, diminishing the human spirit. As many of you know, it is now time to balance the masculine energy with the receptive feminine energies (or you will not be able to evolve and proceed at this time).

The Divine Plan of your planet, Mother Earth, is to learn to "love one another" in equality, harmony, and balance. (Where have you heard that before?) It is your destiny, through your learning choices and freedom of will of separation/duality and lack and limitation, to reconnect from whence you came and to create a wondrous golden-age world of oneness. Dear ones, you can learn to play/interact in oneness while losing the need to either win or compete (an ego mental body attachment and comfort zone).

Once permanently reconnected to Source, together we shall manifest the reality of you humans becoming the master teachers of the multiverse. This is who you truly are and why you are here. Are you ready to know and take ownership of this mighty truth?

We of the Archangelic Realm of Uriel have for eons worked with you and your planet to evolve/advance into your divine destiny. Now is the present moment for all our collected efforts to be. Are you ready yet?

In unconditional love,

Archangel Uriel, loving and connecting you to all the essential aspects of your world and multiverse.

PEACE AND HARMONY

There is a Magic Key in life
That unlocks and releases
The doors of all strife,
Through the Inner God-Power
That can be available
Each and every hour of your day.

The continual adoring and pouring
Of feelings of Peace and Harmony
To all humanity,
Eliminates calamity.

The essential intention of
Feeling Peace, Harmony and Serenity,
Will create ascended eternity.

Fortunate indeed are those
Who have mastered this truth.
Without it,
Humanity has no roof.

So we are speaking of
One of the nice Laws of Life,
In order to allow you to
Manifest Peace and Harmony.

CHAPTER 46

WHAT CAUSED THE DOWNFALL OF PAST GOLDEN AGES?

What Is Affecting Our Next Golden Age?

From Archangel Uriel, World Teacher and Guardian, and Gaia, Mother Earth

Dear Beloved Golden Agers,

It was the **lack of trust and love of higher realms** that created the disconnect from the energies and wisdoms that powered all past six golden ages and caused their demise. This lack of trust and love was a reflection of the relationship with self.

Dear ones, you are now experiencing the final two-thousand-year cycle of your planet in order to create a final golden age of **oneness** that will be supported by the same higher-realm forces as in the past, through your freedom of choice and will, a gift from Source that can never be taken from you. You can ultimately decide which path of learning to choose. You have not always chosen the easy path. Many civilizations throughout the universe do not have a freedom of choice and will; they work directly with Source without question. **You have been given this "gift" as an essential aspect of an experiment in diversity on this planet, to learn to love self, others, and all elements equally.**

Many multiverse forces came together to create your world. It was not created by random evolution, as many believe. When you truly arrive at *the truth of your origin*, this will set you free from many of the belief systems you have now that have kept you in duality and separation.

One of the many forces that came to this planet was the **concept of the human mind**. Within this mind was housed an *alter ego infused with your freedom of choice and will*. This **"mental body" is largely fed by an energy you call the assertive masculine**. Another force you were gifted with was your **"emotional body" fed by an energy you call the receptive feminine**. Since the downfall of your last golden age (Atlantis), you have been struggling ever since **to balance these two masculine and feminine energies.**

The balance of these two creative cosmic forces is essential at this time. Their imbalance is the reason for much of your duality, separation, and confrontation; thus, the need for their balancing.

Prior to the full activation of the mental and emotional bodies, you trusted and loved the higher realms from whence you came and who maintained and sustained your advanced civilizations. You daily allowed yourselves to receive ALL THERE IS. **Then, as an aspect of your divine soul plan, you decided, through your freedom of choice and will, to do it your way**. Over a period of eons, you began to fully not trust (not receive) that there was a Source mightier than yourself giving you all you needed. You then **lost the direct connection completely. An important aspect of your soul plans was to get as far from that Source as possible**, to fully experience life without it, in order to gain your way back to it (coming home).

Dear ones, **the purpose in all this was to prepare you to become the master teachers of this world and universe**. Since you were experiencing every aspect of creation (what is and what is not), you are preparing yourselves for whatever you may need to be *who you are and act upon why you are here*.

So, in effect, **your gift of freedom of choice and will has been your greatest learning tool**. You are now realizing you do not have to learn this way any longer. You are realizing that by **reconnecting, trusting, and loving higher realms**, you can with grace and ease complete your soul plans of master teachership in order to be in service to your world and other worlds.

Through the many messages and teachings that are coming to you during this extraordinary period in your planet's advancing, ascending history, you now **can return to a permanent state of being by fully embodying and embracing your divinity through the creation of your final seventh golden age.**

The reason this will be the final golden age is due to the reality that your planet's time to ascend and return to a body of light has come. Thus, in turn, all upon and within the planet's body will transcend into the higher frequency of light, as well. **You came from light; you shall return to light and then decide what to create again!**

This lesson of trust and love is upon you, dear ones. Those who can integrate that of which we speak now have a marvelous experience ahead of them. Those who do not will take however many lifetimes you need, through your freedom of choice and will, to learn what you need to learn.

What do you choose?

Many of you are weary of the old ways of learning and are ready—**through the trust and love of self, other, all elements on your planet, and higher realms—to create a new paradigm of equality, harmony, and balance.**

Take a deep breath, dear ones, and ask your mental body *to return in service to your knowing, loving heart filled with trust of the WE*. Know, dear ones, **your heart is an outpicturing of the higher realms that have supported and loved you for eons**. Are you ready to trust and love us again as a reflection of your trust and love of self? There is an amazing world for us to cocreate together. Are you ready?

WHAT CREATED OUR LIMITATION

When man became sense conscious
Instead of Creator Conscious
A lack of conscious was created, then.

When hu-MAN-ity began to identify itself
With part of the Whole
Instead of the goal of the Whole,
A new imperfect role began.

Through freedom of choice and will
Mankind soon discovered
Limitation was the result of
The misuse of free will.
Man was now compelled to live
Within his own creation, until...

He soon remembers his noble birth
From the Great Source of All,
Then can choose to reconnect,
And recover from his great Fall.

CHAPTER 47

WHAT IS THE "I AM PRESENCE"? HOW DO WE USE IT?

From Archangel Uriel, World Teacher and Guardian

Dear Beloved Children of Planet Earth,
We world teachers would like to discuss an energetic divine aspect of yourselves called the **I Am Presence.**

The I Am Presence is a frequency vibrating from your heart and soul that lives inside you. It is not something to be brought in from the outside. **The I Am Presence is always present.** It's just a matter of you accessing it. Its energy is most powerfully felt in and around your heart and your throat chakra, where it is expressed in the word.

Your resonance and discernment activate your I Am Presence through your freedom of choice and will. When events flow in your life with grace and ease that is a sure sign you are activating this divine gift and presence.

When humankind's monster of fear, doubt, and ignorance is not present, your I Am Presence is present. When there is no duality, separation, isolation, or conflict, your I Am Presence is present.

Knowing and loving this innermost being will allow complete manifestation of your soul plan (your purpose in being here) and bring you great joy.

It is essential that you begin to know and love this divine aspect of yourself. When you have gratitude for your I Am Presence, great abundance comes forth.

Your I Am Presence is innately gifted to all, a force from creation that allows you to know who you are (a divine being), and why you are here (to be in world service), and where you are headed.

The divine soul whom we are speaking through at this time has compiled a volume of "present phrases" called *The Happiness Handbook: Being Present Is the Present.* This endeavor, which we inspired, will give you further in-depth wisdom concerning your I Am Presence and how to use it.

Being human within the dense 3-D frequency, you are in the process of learning how to accept and access your I Am Presence. A key component to access your I Am Presence is seeing yourself good and worthy enough to receive it. Teachings and tools within the Angel News Network allow you to heal unloving aspects of self in order to fully receive all the abundance life has to offer.

Your I Am Presence allows you to receive "downloads" of your divinity on a regular basis, which raises your vibratory frequency, thus consciousness.

The increased consciousness allows the creation of a new you and world. The word consciousness contains the letters I-O-U (consc-I-O-U-sness). The "I" is "U." This means your consciousness owes you your I Am Presence!

With an open heart, recite after us: I live, move, breathe, and have my being within the invincible strength and power of my mighty I Am Presence, inside me always.

Take a deep breath, dear ones, and on the exhale drop your jaw and release the sound AHH. The sound/vibration AHH connects you with the same frequency/vibration where your I Am Presence eternally lives.

Know through your heart and loving sense of self that you can receive your I Am Presence in each moment of the present. It is your innate divine right. When you fully connect with this presence, you know what it feels like to be free of the unhealed "me" and join the "we."

THE "I AM" PRESENCE

What is this thing, this force called the I AM?
What exactly is present in this name?
A force, a presence that has no shame nor blame.
We hear The Christ, and the name Saint Germain,
Associated with this, the same.

Does anyone truly understand this name,
That has neither shame nor blame?
Let us now attempt to explain…

The I AM seems ancient in its claim
To have created all in this domain.
By the mere spoken word the power of creation
Is released in elaboration.

But since we are part of creation,
This I AM force is part of our self-relation.

The promise of this power
We are told is our, forever more.

Whatever follows the words I AM,
Life forces give mirth to the birth.

I AM first vibrates in the brain,
Followed by the flesh it becomes, the same.

I AM THAT I AM is also my name,
And I can know I am connected to all, with no shame.

It is the imperishable, eternal,
Individual identity of every human being,
Rather than doing, just being.

Perhaps, I AM is just what humanity needs,
To know it is already divine perfection, indeed!

CHAPTER 48

WHAT IS LIFE AND THE TRUE CURE FOR/OF DISEASE?

Adapted by Phillip Elton Collins

D ear Beloved Angel News Network Community,
With so much clearing and cleansing taking place in our bodies at this crucial time, I thought it essential to again discuss the energetic components of life and what within these can effect a cure for the diseases we have and are manifesting. There will come a time when humanity is freed from disease and lives in an immortal state of perfect health. But until that time, allow this "divine discussion" to support our highest good. This life-empowering, medical-altering teaching is adapted from *The Second Coming: The Archangel Gabriel Proclaims a New Age*, by spiritual journalist and author Joel D. Anastasi, channeled by Robert Baker.

The Light of Source never fails.
Phillip Elton Collins

A BRIEF REVIEW: ARCHANGEL GABRIEL DISCUSSES

What are the energetic forces that create life?

What are the true cause and effect of disease that standard medicine does not know or recognize?

Why are we still largely treating symptoms? Are we sure to "cause no harm"?

Why are immune deficiency diseases like cancer and HIV now some of the largest killers in the world?

Most of our current treatments involve "fighting" a disease. What we resist persists. Is there a "neutral" way to heal?

Do we really die or transition into our permanent non-physical form?

Is the human mind the only resource where we can answer the above questions? Are science and our minds ready for solutions that do not come from the human mind, but support our highest good? Has it always been this way during our evolution as a species? Yes, it has!

DNA, THE BASIS OF LIFE

There are sixty-four on-sites in DNA (current science knows forty-four). An on-site is a place in the DNA molecule where a waveform (energy) moves across it connecting two points. In connecting these two points, it produces the amino acids needed to create the chemical interactions in the endocrine system (which we are just beginning to learn the importance of), to bring strength and balance to the immune system and reproduction of the cells to restore the life, balance, and harmony of the physical body. DNA regenerates life. Without these connections, life in the physical cannot continue.

Our bodies renew all their atoms every year. Every few months our skin renews; some of our organs completely reconstruct on an atomic level. This happens through a production of mitosis and reproduction through the instructions of our DNA molecule, since the DNA molecule instructs organisms through the genetic code. So, when the on-sites connect, producing amino acids, it restores health, well-being, and balance to our bodies. Current science has figured out much of this.

When all the DNA on-sites (forty-four to sixty-four) are connected, this will bring about immortality in the physical. This is your destiny as a species, and our science is catching up to the importance of so-called "junk" DNA as the source to this immortality.

THE BODY MEANT TO BE

Your bodies are designed to be healthy and well all the time. Disease is a distortion of the processes of the physical body. Disease is a distortion of the emotional, mental, and physical processes. What we feel and think has a dramatic impact on the physical. Our sciences are also catching up to this reality.

The human body has three energetic diaphragms. There is one in the anus, one in the solar plexus, and one in the throat. A spiral of energy moves up from the base of the spine to your crown (the Kundalini sexual spiral). The other, the erotic spiritual spiral, moves down from the crown to the base. When these forces are unimpeded, it creates a wave called the orgasmic wave through the body, an experience of orgasm that creates a sensation of pleasure and excitement in the body, and supports your desire to be here. This is the life energy itself that current science cannot explain.

When we experience pain or trauma, we begin to shut down our ability to experience those waves of pleasure and excitement for life in order to get rid of or avoid the pain. When this happens, we begin to develop armor rings of blocked energy and blocked emotions in various layers in the body, like layers of an onion. These are horizontal rings, chronically impacted in the muscle tissues, which prevent movement of the pulsation wave up and down in the body to create the sensation of life and pleasure. The pain becomes a "wound" and we develop "ego defenses" to survive/protect the wound. (A discussion of wounds and defenses is an entire teaching in itself, but know that we can identify an individual's wounds and defenses easily and assist in diagnosis and healing.)

Where are these armor rings? There are seven armor rings altogether. There are armor rings in the ocular layers around the eyes and cheekbones; another in the area of the jaw, lips, and tongue; another in the throat, upper shoulders, and neck; another in the chest and arms; and others in the solar plexus, the upper abdominal region, and the pelvis and legs.

HOW AND WHEN ARMOR RINGS DEVELOP

The armor rings develop at various times during childhood development, creating experiences of shutdown with the sexual energy, the erotic force, and the love force (the various energies of life, and lessons unto themselves), restricting the ability to experience the flow of life through the body. This creates a disconnection from our nonphysical, eternal soul and the armoring of the five primary ego defenses. Your ego then maintains and sustains these layers of armored defense chronically in the body. Your body becomes more self-contained as life goes on. You grow into adulthood and shut down more and more, experiencing less pleasure and excitement for life, limiting your life force into a "comfort zone" where you are living or responding to little of life.

Your nervous system then becomes an editing system that edits out everything except what the ego has decided is safe.

So, in effect, we are often living through the illusion of our ego, defending ourselves against life, which stops the flow of energy of the above three forces. The flow of the balance of giving and receiving—the masculine and feminine energies where love and the expression of being connected live—is stopped. We stay in the "me" consciousness, not able to move into "we" consciousness. This is currently changing within our species.

ENERGETIC INFORMATION

The energetic structure of your body is the key element missing in standard medical practice. The body is the vehicle through which the spirit (energy) expresses itself when spirit is awakened (conscious). The energetic spirit aspect of the body cannot be conscious if the body (emotional, mental, and physical) is armored within its processes. The energetic aspect of you is always there—it is not something outside yourself—but it cannot function properly if there are layers of wounds/defenses between you and it.

WHAT CAUSES DISEASE

Through ownership you can begin to ease and free yourselves from disease. All disease is caused by each of you (as a tool to learn what you came here to learn; it is not to make you a victim). All disease is simply caused by imbalances in the functioning of the individual, based upon imbalances in the individual emotionally, mentally, and energetically.

Until you understand and accept that life force (energy) interfered with or interrupted is what creates disease, you will never be able to conquer the illusion of disease in which you currently believe (which is shifting).

Again, life force interruption occurs within your physical body when you have rings of energetic and emotional armoring in the tissues of the body that prevent the life force from flowing freely up through the body. That energy has to go somewhere. If it is confined in a limited space, it attempts to move and interferes with the organs or the areas of the body where it is trapped. There are forms of energetic healing (Reiki, light ascension, hands-on) that greatly assist by allowing the energy to flow properly.

CURRENT MEDICAL COMMUNITY

Your mass medical community has no cognizance of the fact that energy is the source of creation (although this is beginning to change). Therefore, what happens with energy is what creates disease, not what happens with the physical body. The physical body does not create disease. The physical body simply registers disease because it is a hologram or a barometer of what is happening in the areas of creation that produce the physical body.

So, all disease starts energetically, emotionally, and mentally. Then this is translated into the hologram reactions of the physical body. The physical body simply registers symptoms. Thus, the medical profession at large treats symptoms. Its practitioners try to get rid of symptoms. But they don't get to the source of the disease because they do not understand or refuse to understand energy. They do not understand how emotion creates the movement of energy, and thus creates the balance of the immune system and the balance of the conditions of the physical body. And most don't understand or care how the mental belief systems impact the body (our thoughts and emotions create our reality; that's how powerful we are). Your thoughts and emotions can actually be stored within your DNA cellular memory. Since they are not curing most diseases, some doctors are opening themselves to the new truth here. Let's be careful and not kill the messengers of new truths, as in the past. Let's accept with compassion and forgive what we do not know and where we need to change.

CANCER AND HIV

More people die of cancer and HIV than ever before. Cancer has become the leading killer in America, overtaking heart disease. Your cure rate with these diseases is low, since you do not yet fully understand the cause/problem. Any immune deficiency disease is created on a cellular level. It involves the cellular reproduction of the body. Therefore, this disease, at its source, is a problem or a trauma that basically involves shame of self on a very primitive cellular level. This shame is often the result of not accepting who you are through self-identity. It is the lack of a loving relationship with self (the way in which people use the force of creation in their lives to experience and express the power and identity of who they are).

Sexual identity issues are often seen in cancer and HIV. Cancer often strikes women (breast/reproductive organs) and men (prostate) related to their sexual identity. HIV is a sexually transmitted disease related to one's sexual identity. It is related to energy that is blocked that does not allow the cellular memory of the body to reproduce itself at a healthy rate. It influences production of the T-cells, which reproduce the physical body.

THE CURES

To better address the cures for these diseases, which produce deterioration of the physical body largely based upon shame and a lack of self-love, you need to get to the core. You need to get to the issues of shame and a lack of self-love on a cellular level, where the right to be, the right to have life, the right to be you, is concerned. These issues have to be cleared. The traumas locked in certain regions of the body have to be cleared. The energy then has to flow through the body, because the energy flows in the body determine the rate at which the cells can reproduce.

All the emotional memories of shame and a lack of self-love are taught/programmed into the spiritual aspect of the DNA at a very early age. This is encoded in the DNA, which is what makes it a cellular disease and one of immune deficiency, because immune deficiency comes from the inability of the connecting points in the DNA to connect. When this happens, they cannot produce the amino acids to create the chemical interactions needed for the reproduction of cellular memory to restore the physical body. When that process breaks down, when the sense of self is shamed, it affects the immune system.

THE IMMUNE SYSTEM

The immune system is not created to fight anything. Most disease cures are set up on the premise of fighting something. What you resist persists. The immune system is created to assimilate the experiences of life. When it is forced to fight, it breaks down. This affects the production of cells. Therefore, the source of the emotion has to be gotten to. There is a reason cancer and HIV are so rampant in our society. It is based upon shame of self that produces lack of intimacy and connection. This is reflected in our wars, politics, marriage and divorce rates, and our dualistic civilization, where it is often every man for himself.

You are in the process of learning that without equality and unity you cannot advance as a species and survive. There are several new therapeutic processes that allow you to heal needs to be healed.

NEW THERAPIES

New therapeutic processes have been created to allow the necessary flow of energy throughout the body by releasing the emotional and mental programming that's trapped in the muscle tissues and organs. This trapped energy creates the energetic armoring that blocks the energy flow throughout the body.

These processes work like this. Each energetic construction is based upon where and how the energy is armored in the body. As stated earlier, there are seven rings of armoring. Each one of those layers is related to a state of development in childhood. Each of those has consecutive layers of energetic armoring that create tension and stress in a certain area of the body and block the flow of energy there. When the energy is blocked, it cannot flow through the body, so it literally explodes because it is locked in. This predetermines what areas of the body later in life will probably break down and become diseased—heart, digestion, arthritis, cancer, HIV, etc.

What happens depends upon where the predominant layers of armoring are based, the particular defense structure of the person, and which levels of emotional development the child locked into.

HOW WE OFTEN DEAL WITH DISEASE AND NO MORE NEED FOR IT

Humans largely deal with disease on a physical level, discounting energy's role. So you often deal with disease on a level of microbes, viruses, and cellular balance and imbalance. What you do not yet fully understand is that if you got at the source of how disease is created from the perspective of movements of energy, you would no longer be working with physical symptoms. When you work with the flows of energy, you will not have disease anymore. It is your destiny that this takes place in your evolution.

HOW WE SHALL FREE OURSELVES FROM DISEASE

As humans begin to fully understand the functioning of DNA and how to manipulate this, you will be able to eliminate disease altogether. Remember that DNA is the cellular structure recording all the information that moves through the body. The DNA holds not just the physical genetic implications but also the emotional, mental, and energetic patterns. Basically, DNA is a blueprint of patterns that the RNA has sent it. The

RNA records the information from the body and sends it into the DNA. The DNA unscrambles it and sorts it into blueprints or patterns. In the past, the RNA molecule has been functioning in one way only. It sends information to the DNA from the body system and through the endocrine system (which mirrors the star systems that seeded this planet).

As we begin to open the spiritual (energy) aspect of DNA, it begins to operate as a two-way system. In the future, it will begin to send information it has recorded in the DNA out into the consciousness of the individual. So we will be able to access what is recorded in the DNA on a conscious level and begin to manipulate that. This will be a life-altering game-changer for how we live!

WHAT TO DO UNTIL WE KNOW MORE

Until the above information becomes commonplace, stay connected to like-minded/spirited people, gaining a greater understanding of how your own physical body operates and taking responsibility for balancing its energy flows. You can raise the vibration of your body, overcome disease, and maintain your body in balance and health. You can also begin to share with others what you know. Studying Reiki energetic healing is one method whereby you begin to understand energy: how to access it, how to make it flow, and how to balance it.

The more we investigate the origins of life from the energetic standpoint, the more it becomes something that people embrace, the more it becomes common knowledge and less mysterious and threatening to established medicine. Then we can develop comprehensive/integrated medicine.

Reiki (energetic) healing is a method of learning to use the universal life force of energy. But that is not enough. You also have to have an understanding of your own personal process (which requires a deep examination of your relationship with self). When the author took his training as a healing arts therapist, he had to be in a personal process so he could better receive his healing in order to assist others in theirs. Participating in a therapeutic process is necessary because the vehicle must be clear in order to sustain the movement of energy. One of the reasons there is so much diseases on our planet, so many immune-deficiency diseases, is because there are great imbalances in our physical systems.

THE TRUTH ABOUT GERMS

Many of you were taught that germs create disease. Since then, science has reversed that, saying germs do not create disease. Germs can contribute to creating imbalance, but they do not create disease. You are exposed to germs all the time. You have germs in your body constantly. Why do some people take those germs and create disease and others do not? It has nothing to do with the germs; it has to do with how the body is responding to what is taking place, how it is using it.

Take the immune system, for instance; people have thought the immune system is used to fight disease. It does not fight disease. When the immune system has to fight, it breaks down. It is used for bringing balance to the body. When the immune system is balanced, there is health and well-being. When it is out of balance because it has to fight, it breaks down, and disease occurs because it becomes weakened.

ENERGIES OF THE PLANET AND OUR BODY

The energies of the planet have been raising their vibration over the past seventy-five years, particularly since 1987 (on the author's birthday), when the Harmonic Convergence occurred. This created a massive step-up of that vibration. Since then, the Jupiter comet occurrence in 1994 and other cosmic events have taken place. Each has created an infusion of higher vibration of consciousness and energy into the Earth plane and the bank of DNA around the Earth. This is creating a mutation of the planetary DNA and also creating a mutation of the human DNA.

Because of these events, and because your bodies are so polluted or blocked, when the vibration is raised it starts an entrainment process that brings up everything that is diseased in the body, everything that is out of balance, everything that is in resistance, everything that is in conflict. Does this sound like our world today? And the body simply becomes a mirror of the conflict!

When you start this entrainment process, all your "stuff" comes to the surface and all the toxins start to surface. So you go through a kind of healing crisis because you are disturbing energetic blocks within your body that have been there for years. Most of you have learned to live with this with a certain degree of stress and shutdown, and you have accepted it as normal or part of growing old.

The experience of humanity is not one of becoming more open and available to life. The process of living, aging, and getting older has become a process of gradually shutting down to life. This has become the normal process, quite the reverse of what it should or is intended to be.

There is no reason why the body has to age and fall apart. The only reason it does is because as you grow older (because of your wounds and defenses), you shut off to more and more life. And you often create a smaller and smaller frame of reference for living. You often fight change, fight development, and fight growth.

You humans often seem to accept limitation and lack rather than growth, expansion, and development because change appears threatening. But the process of living is the process of changing. The process of living from a soul/energy perspective is the process of growth and expansion. That's all your soul is interested in! Your wounded ego is interested in confining, limiting, and keeping things in a comfort zone that it can understand and attempt to control.

By allowing the ego, housed within your belief system's mental bodies, to surrender to your knowing hearts, you can allow yourselves to surrender to not knowing and allow the void to reveal all possibilities and probabilities of life—a new way of being and healing.

BREATH SOUND AND MOTION

How much you are able to breathe in determines how much life you feel you deserve, how much of life you are able to receive. This is a direct indication of your receiving pattern. How much you breathe out is going to be determined by how much you breathe in. So it is an exact indication of your ability to give of yourself, to share yourself, and to expose yourself to life.

How you breathe is the key to how you live. This is the fundamental key to the universe; it is the key to life.

As much as you are able to breathe in is as much of life as you are able to receive—that you feel you have a right to receive. Therefore, you will limit yourself to receiving life according to how much you limit your breath. If you limit your taking in of life, you will also be limiting what you feel you have to give to life, what you feel you can be exposed to life, what you feel you can give to life without feeling you are giving up something or giving yourself.

Giving and receiving are the exact mirror of each other. In effect, they are the same thing. As you give, you receive. As you receive, you give. If you are only breathing out, only giving, you will die. If you are only breathing in, only taking, you will die. You must be able to breathe in and out. Most people use only 15–20 percent of their lung capacity. This is an indication of how much you feel you deserve where life is concerned and how healthy you are.

You are literally living a life of starvation. You are starving the brain of oxygen and its capacity to function as a physical unit to be able to interpret and take in consciousness. This is why most people are not very astute where conscious awareness is concerned. They are asleep because the brain itself is not oxygenated, so it cannot fire neutrons.

Being able to breathe in, or not, also interferes with the functioning of the endocrine system. The endocrine system is the distributor of energy to the various chemical processes that nourish and nurture the organs and systems of the body. It is the doorway between the conscious mind, the subconscious, and the superconscious.

Breathing controls the functioning of the nervous system through how it balances or distorts the serotonins and various chemical processes that are produced in the brain. The breath is also the source of the reproduction of life on a cellular level. The breath is the source of all this!

You have been given the gift of life in the breath, the secret of life in the breath. If you use that secret of life, you have the ability to regenerate life endlessly. The one thing that keeps you from regenerating life and reproducing it, which results in aging, disease, and death, is in fact that less than 1 percent of the body can reproduce itself. The cells of the body are programmed with messages of trauma and therefore stimulate the release of the emotional charges held in the body that keep the damaged areas in place.

If, on the other hand, you are able to free yourselves from your personal history in the body, you have the potential of immortality in the physical body.

BACK TO DNA AND IMMORTALITY

Scientists have called the forty-four on-sites that have never been stimulated the junk DNA, but they're beginning to understand that it is not junk DNA. It is spiritual DNA. It is the potential for immortality in the physical. As they further uncover the secret to the DNA molecule, they are now predicting the possibility of the average life span increasing to two hundred years over the next fifty to one hundred years. And within the next two hundred to five hundred years, they are predicting the average life span increasing up to five hundred or more years.

These are speculations based upon what scientist have discovered thus far. However, those speculations fall far short of what is possible. Look at the cases where a life-threatening disease has had an instantaneous healing. That healing happened because more than twenty on-sites in the DNA were activated. By activating a few more on-sites, the disease was eradicated from the body instantaneously. If you were using ten more of those on-sites on a regular basis, think what could be possible.

As discussed earlier, incorporating personal processing and breathing, you further access the sensation of being. Remember, you stop breathing because breathing produces feeling. And feeling is the sensation of the movement of the life energy through the body.

When the movement of that life energy through feeling is associated with pain, you begin to stop the breath process to stop pain. This begins early in childhood and gradually increases into adolescence. By the time you are an adult, you have pretty much begun a slow movement toward annihilation simply through the process of shutting off feeling.

The DNA molecule is influenced by feeling. It holds all your emotional patterns of resistance and acceptance in place. When you are holding feelings in the body, you are holding the life force and preventing it from movement, preventing it from having expression. When this happens, it creates a length of waveform in the DNA that misses connecting the on-sites.

Therefore, it does not produce the necessary amino acids and chemical production in the endocrine system that brings about the balance in the immune system. So when you are holding emotions, you are having a negative experience of emotion because holding or suppressing creates resistance, which creates pain. Pain creates fight, and any form of fighting or resistance stimulates a closed system that is feeding upon itself and the system breaks down.

When, however, the DNA is affected by a wave of movement of feeling, which means you are accepting and experiencing your feeling moment to moment, it produces a different length of waveform. It is a matter of allowing all feelings, negative or positive. The DNA is stimulated by the allowance of all feelings. When there is a flow of feelings, it produces a length of waveform that connects the on-sites in the DNA molecule. Connecting those on-sites produces and stimulates the production of those chemicals needed to bring about the balance of the immune system, and thus, the physical body.

Remember, the entire process starts with your breathing; breathing is the source. Without breathing you cannot think or feel, because breathing awakens the consciousness in the physic body. When you breathe into the body, you stimulate awareness. You stimulate life. You stimulate consciousness. So the physical body, the emotional body, and the mental body are dependent upon the breath. Everything in life is dependent on three things: the breath, movement, and sound. Life is movement. Resistance is not moving, which is death.

HEALING

All healing is a manifestation of knowing on some level—the ability to know the perfect state of being and to hold that perfect state unflinchingly, without doubt. To hold it with the wholeness of your being, with absolute knowing of the perfection of that state of well-being and health. To focus not on the disease, but on the healing. Not even on the healing so much, because when you focus on the healing, you are focusing on the expectation of process rather than the knowing of the state of being.

When you encounter a disease such as cancer, allow yourself to embody the truth of that life force; to embody it by becoming neutral, taking it within, allowing it to pass through you, and allowing it to radiate forth to those who will receive it.

Worry simply adds to the problem. It sustains the cancer. Worry is not love. It is fear. See yourself or another in a perfect state of being, without doubt. Move into the quantum field of possibility and probability, which is the pregnant void of creation. It is the place of all probability and possibility that exists simultaneously at all times. (Doubt, fear, and ignorance are the monsters of mankind.)

When you dip into the seas of possibility and probability where reality is concerned, let yourself be sure to dip into it with a very clear focus of that intention, so that you pull from it the probability that you want to create most specifically.

Focus your consciousness, your feelings, and your intentions. You can surround the cancer cells with absolute love. Embrace them with absolute acceptance, nurturing, and love so that you are not fighting them. Because the minute you have to fight anything, you are aiding and abetting the very thing you want to destroy.

Affirm that you are in a perfect state of health and well-being. That it is your divine right; demand and declare that it is as it is. You are perfect here and now. Divine love always has met and always will meet every human need.

Begin to approach life and disease in a different way. In doing so, you will approach life and disease in a way that has faith in life, trust in life, and that honors life through the choices you make in life that are different from the ones you are making now.

LIGHT DEFINED

Light is matter, energy and luminosity,
One in all three,
So you can see light.
That makes up, and wakes up
The eternal spiritual body, all right.

This immortal light body is
Composed and condenses,
In a sense,
By your I AM Presence, in residence,
Which is self-maintaining and sustaining,
Ever expanding, ever perfect purpose,
And the catchall of divine light,
Truth and Power
From the very heart-center of creation.

This white light body,
Is your eternal, individuated
Lyre of life, and heartfelt center
Of manifested form.

In its present form,
We can only behold, not hold this holy form,
Not even for a half-second of a second.

But someday soon, if we so choose,
We shall ascend into,
This white body of light,
And leave never more.

CHAPTER 49

WHEN WILL YOU BECOME WISE THROUGH WISDOM?

Codes of Wisdom

From Archangel Uriel, World Teacher and Guardian

Dear Beloved Knowing Humans,
You *think* you know many things within your world. Dear ones, you do know more than you ever have known before, but is your world improving and behaving like an advanced civilization? Even though there are still more untruths than truths in your world, and much of the reality of your world is yet to be revealed, some of the mysteries of life are being revealed in an attempt to prevent you from destroying yourselves. **The core issue is that you have much knowledge but little applied wisdom. Wisdom is collected knowledge over**

periods of time and applied through discernment in the moment it is needed. The basic reason for this shortfall is that most of you do not recognize or believe in repeated lives on Earth, and you have allowed the human mind, powered by assertive masculine energy, to continue to control. It is time for the mind to move into service to the feminine energy heart, and allow the masculine and feminine energies to balance. All advanced civilizations rely on the accumulated knowledge into applied wisdom over many lifetimes through the wisdom of their hearts.

In spite of all your so-called knowledge, without applied wisdom, you have not yet created communities of equality, harmony, and balance throughout your world. You have more of your species enslaved than ever before. You still accept the concept of war and killing one another as an acceptable alternative to a dispute. You still abuse your planet, selves, and one another to the point of near destruction. All this is the result and lack of applied wisdom and love.

When are you going to alter the reality you are creating by applying the knowledge you already have? You have enough knowledge to know what works and what does not, and what is best for the good of all. And yet you continue your destructive ways.

There are old patterns of behavior (the hidden few controlling the many) that are beginning to shift. Dear ones, there are more of you than the ones controlling you! When are you going to stop giving your power away to those who do not have your highest good in place? The answer is, dear ones, the day you **wake up and realize you love you and are worthy of another choice, and act upon it.**

The word wisdom comes from the phrase "wise dominion." *The dominion is dominion over self* by choosing to rise above and beyond the old and create the new. **Wisdom lives within your hearts and is easily accessed through self-empowerment and love**. If you choose, it is time to move beyond controlling, untrue belief systems that limit and separate, and embrace new paradigms that support your divine soul plans to move into Oneness.

Your closed hearts are what is creating so much dis-ease within your world. Closed hearts separate through fear (absence of love) and create duality and confrontation. It is time to open your wise hearts and access the wisdom that lies within, and apply it throughout your weary, waiting world.

The encoded wisdom stored within your heart's DNA from many lifetimes will allow you to access all the knowledge you need. You simply have to surrender and trust that it is there, and ask for it to support you. Ask and ye shall receive.

Dear ones, stop and take a deep breath, connect with your heart, and ask for the wisdom of your heart to be imparted to you. There has been so much suffering in your world by denying incarnational reality and the divine use of you heart; the heart knows, the mind believes.

Let us now review the THIRTY CODES OF WISDOM to become masters of wisdom:

*   There are children here DNA equipped to way show humanity; love and protect them

*   Wisdom often comes in unlikely individuals; honor all you meet

* Be not silent in wisdom; it is the foundation of truth

* There are karmic consequences when wisdom is not lovingly applied

* Wisdom prevents fear, doubt, and ignorance; the monsters of humanity

* Learn to think and listen with your heart; it is the organ that houses wisdom

* Following your heart allows wisdom to activate your divine soul plan (reason to be here)

* Wisdom builds communities of equality, harmony, and balance

* Wisdom eliminates shaming, blaming, and judgment

* Wisdom often resides within silence, inaction, or reaction

* If wisdom brings you greatness, return it in gentleness and humility

* Honoring another's wisdom is the true path to a friend

* Wisdom is the great storehouse of ALL THERE IS

* Knowledge can reflect ignorance and create the fool; wisdom is a shared friend

* The wise person allows the heart to open with the mouth shut

* Wisdom is the frequency of cosmic light; mysteries revealed

* Wisdom overcomes all things

* Wisdom may come from different sources, but offers the same vision

* Wisdom is the pathway to freedom for any and all bondage or separation

* Wisdom will lead humanity to Oneness

* Wisdom teaches all that exists is only another form of that which does not exist

* Wisdom is the way through illusion

* Wisdom is the medicine of awakening and healing dis-ease

* Wisdom is formless yet forming

* Wisdom is infinite wisdom

* Wisdom is known yet unknown

* Wisdom holds the key to all magic

* Wisdom is the cure for so-called death; moving you into eternity

* Wisdom frees the mind, and allows it to move back into service to the heart, allowing the soul to move into spirit

* Wisdom is within you, not outside yourself; knowledge is outside self

Dear ones, are you ready through these codes to take a vow to become masters of wisdom?

BELIEF AND KNOWING

The mind believes,
The heart knows,
So sayeth, our soul.

Beliefs change,
But truth remains the same,
Is the game.

Those who intend to know,
Will know.

Those who believe often
Get locked into a mindset
That is difficult to unset
And can cripple their ability
To see beyond the net of the mind,
Often eluding truth's upset.

You are the one deciding your destiny,
Through freedom of choice and will.
So keep your mind and heart open.
Ask questions, explore the unknown,
Until it becomes the known.

Now the mind is moving
Back into service to the heart,
Being vice versa for a long time,
Knowing where that got us.

Now we shall experience truth,
Without being thrown
Under the bus!

CHAPTER 50

WHO GETS TO GOVERN?

From the Archangelic Realm of Uriel

Dear Beloved Humans being governed,

Governments always reflect and mirror the people they are governing. If you so choose, it is time to really look at the universal truth, dear ones. Most of your world, including the countries you call a democracy, are not living in equality, harmony, and balance. Why exactly is this? Because of each of you and your unhealed relationship with yourself. If you so choose, it is time to know this and begin to apply many of the tools and teachings that are coming to you from higher realms.

Within higher realms, none gain the opportunity to govern another unless they have reached a certain degree of healing within themselves that allows that to reflect out onto those they govern and support. There is not room for deceit or denial of the deceit, which fills your governments and world, dear ones. Of course, our being telepathic and knowing what others are thinking (your divine destiny) prevents untruths from being in our world. But until you have earned and evolved into telepathy, there are some reminders that can take place now to assist and support you in the present moment.

This is not to say there are not some well-intended people in your governments. There are, dear ones. It's just that their efforts are so overshadowed within a corrupted system; they seldom can fully succeed.

Let's return to the cause and effect of what exists at present. Most humans believe that one person can achieve little in changing things, **instead of realizing it all starts with ONE, since you are all ONE**. If you can begin to imagine and then know that you are all aspects of the same thing, that just might change how you treat yourself and one another, and change who you wish to elect into a government office.

Dear ones, you have an inner gyro system called **resonance and discernment** that can allow you to know who and what is true and better suited to govern your world. This is an eternal gift from your higher self to assist you in creating and choosing to create a higher frequency/consciousness government, thus world.

Can you see many of those who are attempting to control you and your governments now are destroying your very home, your planet, and making many of your lives miserable due to a lack of equality, harmony, and balance? **You are not here to suffer, dear humans**, even though some old-paradigm religions told you so. Only a lack of self-love and truth can continue to hold this old belief in place.

As you have been taught in the past, this planet is **a divine experience of learning to love**, a Lover-versity, if you will. The planet was created from the energies of twelve star systems that seeded it. Each of these star systems brought unique gifts to the process. Your races, genders, geographic locations, languages, and cultures throughout your world reflect this intended diversity. There are portals and vortices throughout your planet that attract certain expressions of diversity. What has happened particularly in some of your large land masses, like your so-called China, Russia, and Brazil, where there is a wide expression of diversity, your man-made governments have attempted—through dictatorships, autocratic, and so-called communist governments—to control the people. As your history has demonstrated, these attempts at control are short-lived and will continue to be so. When the people under these corrupted governments continue their wake up, **all will continue their soul paths to oneness, allowing the evolutionary path of each nation**. And a word regarding those who attempt to harm or prevent the destiny of humanity, the universe knows quite well how to balance imbalance through karma.

One of the major reasons that the **United States of America**, as a large land mass, chose the path it did had to do with the cycle of ascension taking place on the planet. This country was chosen to be the **"heart of the world,"** leading the planet to its divine destination of oneness. The founding fathers of the United States of America were divinely led through the creation of the documents from which the country was formed. The manifestation of so-called America is not complete, but continues to be in process; not perfected/manifested yet, but way showing.

Let us speak about **control** for a moment, dear ones. **Humanity is not in control of anything**. You may think you are, but you are not. **You cannot be in control of**

things you did not create (this is a universal law). You did not create your world or the life upon it. The sooner you master this truth, the easier your transition into higher-frequency reality will be. In your past and present religions, the first governing bodies transformed into what you call governments and corporations. All of these man-made structures have attempted to control you through their wounded mental, largely assertive masculine energies. Since control is an illusion, and there is no control, you may ask what is there? What is there, dear ones, is a frequency, a consciousness that created you, but doesn't intend nor can control you since it is not part of the human mind. This Creator gave you freedom of choice and will that, like itself, no one nor nothing can disrupt.

You are here to wake up, to love self and others, and to know your divine destiny as eternal beings of light in human form; to become the master teachers of the universe! Nothing less will be and do, dear ones.

So how did the present existence of your world come to be (knowing it is in the process of shifting into a magnificent new)? As explained earlier, this all was and is **an agreement** you made to learn what you need to learn to finally BE who you are and know why you are here. And this has largely been achieved through **experiencing** *what is not in order to know what is.* **Humans love to learn this way. In fact, it is often the only way you can learn.**

The messenger through whom we are coming to you at this divine time is a brethren within an endeavor called the Angel News Network, whose mission (like many others) is to bring teachings and tools from higher realms beyond the human mind to you. *The intention of these messages is to raise your frequency, thus consciousness, which will assist in your self-empowerment and healing of the wounded me transforming into the healed we of world service (your reason to be here).*

It is time, dear ones, humanity becomes conscious of the forces that created it, and continue to maintain and sustain your world and selves, through your reunion with creation, which can, with grace and ease, help you transcend into your divine destiny and resume your rightful place with all higher realms. Remember, you agreed to experience all this to become who you are: **the master teachers of the universe**.

Dear ones, the Archangelic Realm of Uriel, and all other higher realms, are so grateful for the choices humanity has made. We recognize it has not been an easy journey, but we know it has been a necessary pathway through your freedom of will and choice. When you reascend into your reunion with us, it will be like the mother during childbirth. At the actual birth, all the pain (not suffering) is forgotten when the infant connects to the mother's breast. That's what you will be doing, dear ones, reconnecting yourselves to the forces that fathered and mothered you! This is the force of which we are all in service! You are in your final Earth cycle for this to take place. The time line will be determined based upon each one's soul plan.

ENDING WAR: THE NEXT GOLDEN AGE

It is furious folly for one part
Of God's creation
To war against another part.

When will you know
War simply does not work!

Confrontation is the height
Of selfishness and lack of self-love,
Creating bondage and misery
Where there can be no peace of the dove.

Awaken weary world
And know
Soon you will bless your sisters and brothers,
Rather than wage wrongful war.

Learning what is
From what is not
Is done.

For the time of duality and separation
Is through
As you know the true you,
As Children of Earth

Sent here for preparation,
To now end duality and separation, forever more...

Now focus on creating your next Golden Age,
And remember,
You are destined to be
The Master Teachers and senders
Of Liquid White Light and Love,
Throughout the Universe,
In Oneness, for ages more...

CHAPTER 51

WHO IS ARCHANGEL URIEL?

From the Archangelic Realm of Uriel

Dear Beloved Human Brothers and Sisters,

We come to you at this most crucial path in your planetary and personal human evolution, entering your divine destiny, to further explain who we are, the frequency of consciousness you call Archangel Uriel, and our eternal love and support of your planet and all people. **Our name Uriel means "The Light of God," and we have ancient and deep ties to your Earth and humanity.**

Dear ones, long before your world and humanity existed, we have been in service to ALL THERE IS, the Creator, Source, God—whatever name of which you resonate or not. For whether you believe or know we exist, we do.

There are many higher-realm beings that have always existed beyond the denser frequency in which you now reside and of which you are ascending. From your frequency point, unseen beings such as Earth-bound elementals, Inner Earth

313

civilizations (inside your planet), angels and archangels (serving humanity), intergalactic beings (who act as a liaison between denser and higher frequencies), star systems (that seeded your planet), and universal and multiverse councils (just to name a few), have always been working toward the highest good of your planet and all living things (including you) upon, within, and above your Earth.

You are in the process of remembering that your world is much more expansive than you ever were taught or imagined. **We of Uriel are one of an unlimited arena of realms that serve Creation**, and often serve you, through unconditional love. We are forever joining the macrocosm with the microcosm.

Not to overwhelm you with names (which we really don't have, since we do not have language as you know it) and responsibilities, let us singularly focus on the frequency in which we of Uriel reside. There are many teachings available to you concerning the other higher realms of which we speak. The names we are about to use regarding Uriel are those humanity has created and adopted to better know us. If they resonate, use them; if not, create names of your own, dear ones. The purpose of this exploration is to further identify ourselves so our hearts, minds, and hands may join in oneness.

There are many levels of angels and archangels within this solar system and galaxy. **We of the Archangelic Realm of Uriel are one the four major archangels (Gabriel, Michael, Raphael) whose assignment, if you will, is to serve humanity**. *While never having been human, we maintain and sustain essential aspects of your mental, emotional bodies, your thoughts, feelings, and consciousness, in order to support the divine* *distribution of the universal flow (power) and how that supports all aspects of the Earth's environment, especially you.*

In effect, we are humanity's link to the higher spiritual realms that can show you how to connect with your inner self-empowerment (self-mastery), which is the tool to help you individually shift in consciousness, thus accelerate the whole of humanity into higher realms of consciousness. No small order, dear ones.

While working closely with the **Christ Consciousness energies, the Mary feminine energies, and the Great White Brotherhood** (path of personal Christhood), we of Uriel are often referred to as the **Great Archangel of the Earth** and are in selfless service to Creation and humanity. We can show you how to take ownership of all the aspects of your lives you have chosen through your divine soul plans to learn what you came here to learn—turning victimhood into ownership, transforming disappointments into freedom—knowing there is victory and blessings in 3-D adversities. We of Uriel can assist you in clearing and cleansing feelings and thoughts of the past and present trapped within your cellular DNA, allowing your acceptance and compassion of self, thus unconditional forgiveness (penetrating each plane until it reaches the physical).

Beloveds, **we bring the power of unconditional forgiveness of self and others to humanity as the key to entering higher energetic vibration and consciousness: the penetration of the divine force to the physical plane. This will set you free!**

As Archangel Michael uses his sword to assist you in moving from your mind to your heart, we of Uriel also use a *flaming sword to purify mental and emotional understanding (that has been creating your dense reality) that transmutes lower vibrational energies into enlightened spiritual understanding.*

We now once again speak with you during this sacred time of ascension upon your planet and your willingness to embrace the shift into higher consciousness. Dear ones, are you ready to listen, act, and transcend the human experience? We stand ever present to assist you in every area of your lives.

TELLING THE TRUTH

Think of the money and time
We could save
If everyone was telling the truth.

And never mind not being able to trust,
With such little truth in the roost.

The world is filled with deceit,
And the denial of that deceit.
It's become a not so neat cultural norm,
To twist another's arm.

Through the evolution of consciousness
We are breaking down old controls,
And old paradigm roles,
Those no longer apply.

Even ancient scrolls are new again
Revealing what needs to be healed again,
In the now.

The ancient truths teach and tell
That being true, or not,
Reveals the real you.

Archangelic, Inner Earth and Star Realms, too,
Are now assisting in creating the new,
Telling the truth,
All the time.

CHAPTER 52

CURRENT CURRENCIES

From Archangel Uriel, World Teacher and Guardian

Dear Beloved Humans,
    Your world financial systems are based upon deceit and denial of that deceit, with a very few controlling the entire system. Until this truth is revealed and accepted worldwide and you create a new transparent system based upon truth, you will remain with the same, no matter what you call it. The entire concept of abundance and monetary systems is in need of truly being evaluated. Your currencies are really IOUs based upon myth and credit. Most economies are consumed in what you call debt, based upon the illusion that something really exists. The debt allows control. Humanity is partially attempting to create a new paradigm, but the old is holding on for dear life to continue to deceive and control. You know what you have really isn't working, but you don't know exactly what to be/do about it. Truth and transparency are what is needed in your world now. Where you are headed, into higher realms, there is no need for the systems you have in place now. It is your destiny to create/ manifest through the purity of self exactly what you need.

TRUE WEALTH

Man "thinks" he controls his true wealth,
He hoards it, and keeps it even from self,
Keeping much more than he needs,
So others may not feed.

In his illusion man allows one percent
To control and withhold
Ninety-nine percent of the whole.

Only when man knows and understands
That the Great God-Self is the only
Real owner and controller of all wealth
Can he free himself from the me,
To consciousness of the we.

All wealth comes from the Earth, somehow,
And belongs to our Mother,
Who merely wishes that we share
With our sister and brother.

You have been shown
Who really governs the world's wealth?
Let this be the individual's soul test,
To see if you will and can share it with the rest...

CHAPTER 53

YOUR TALENTS
AND GIFTS

From Archangel Uriel, World Teacher and Guardian

Dear Humans Being Talented and Gifted,

Here's *the divine deal*, dear ones: as cosmic eternal beings of light, *you have been given talents and gifts that are essential fragments of your soul plans*. Within each incarnational cycle you have learned, or not, *how to bring these out into world service*; to demonstrate who you are and show why you are here. The world and universe are incomplete without the full expressions of these within you. In effect, *they make the world and universe go round*.

There have been many reasons through various wounds and defenses why you have or have not been able to bring these gifts and talents out into the world. We of higher realms have gifted you many tools and teachings to allow you to access your talents and gifts (see Life Mastery, www.theangelnewsnetwork.com). When they are activated, your feel a great joy and know your purpose in being here. **Are you ready to access**

whatever is within yourselves to bring the unique greatness of you forward?

Your world and yourselves are involved in an extraordinary process called ascension, where your home planet is raising her frequencies to return to being a body of light; thus, all within and upon her body will be of the same frequency or be relocated elsewhere. There is a great opportunity and need for all your talents and gifts to come forward, for every one of you are the *manifestors* of your future. Without your talents and gifts, you are missing the opportunity to create communities of equality, harmony, and balance. If you so choose, through your freedom of choice and will, we invite you to heal whatever needs to be healed within yourselves in order to bring your talents and gifts out into the world, which will make an essential difference. **It all begins individually inside, with each one of you bringing it outside—a process of inside out, not outside in.**

We higher realms know only too well what a special ascension opportunity is being afforded humanity. **You are each being given the opportunity and tools to show to the world** your desire to be in **world service** through your cosmic talents and gifts. You are uncovering and discovering that you are more amazing than you ever imagined, dear ones.

We of the Archangelic Realm of Uriel are watching to see who stands up and is willing to make a difference; who has enough compassion and love for themselves to reflect that out into the world, to see you are all one, and begin to free yourselves from all the lack, limitation, and duality of the past and present. **Know you are not alone in this endeavor**, dear ones. You have always had the love and support of higher realms. Are you ready to fully receive us now by simply asking for what you need?

Within each of your hearts is the DNA of your talents and gifts. With every beat, your heart is asking you to bring the true you out into the world. You are all teaching what you need to learn in order to heal self and your world, and to become the master teachers of the universe.

Dear ones, **we are all divine beings on a sacred journey**. Do you choose to ascend to the full frequency of your divine self or stay in the world you see around you? As you awaken to embody your eternal divine self, remember that you are the only one who can prevent or achieve success.

It is time to be fearless (in complete love of self and others) and bring your creative, innovative talents and gifts into the world. This will shift things, releasing, not fighting (what you resist persists) the old, but allowing the new paradigm of equality, harmony, and balance to organically flow parallel to the old and replace it (sometimes quickly, sometimes gradually).

Success is yours for the taking, through your self-empowered talents and gifts. Let us join our eternal oneness and be the divine beings of light we are.

Know, dear ones, the light is your heritage and true home; know that by experiencing the absence of light you can now lift the veil of darkness that has been your teaching tool. Sealed within your heart is the eternal brightness you can choose to shine out into the world now through your talents and gifts.

You are children of the stars, sons and daughters of the Sun. Know that wherever you inhabit you are One with the stars. Your emotional, mental, and physical

bodies are like planets revolving around your soul, the Sun. As you are again remembering your talents and gifts, they will shine into the darkness and you will see and be one with the light again.

Dear ones, you are not of the Earth, but a child of the Conscious Cosmic Light; your talents and gifts were born here. Once you remember this, you will know your mother and father are the light. You then can finish healing yourselves and world, and move into your master teachership of the universe.

OUR GREATNESS

Humankind walks in the forgetting of our Greatness,
Not remembering what Power and Knowledge lies
within each of our souls.

We walk through Life unaware of our Talents and Gifts,
Seeking secrets already known within us.

We are Eternal Beings of Light,
Awaiting our Awakening and En-light-en-ment.

Wisdoms once known will now awaken
Within each of us in World Service,
If we so choose in our observance.

All that ever was and still is
Is waiting to be born in WE CONSCIOUSNESS,
If we can just get the me out of the we,
Creating worlds of equality, and harmony.

Are you ready?
I AM.

CHAPTER 54

YOUR HIGHER SELF ALREADY KNOWS

From Archangels Gabriel, Michael, Raphael, and Uriel

Dear Beloved Human Beings,

* Truth is constant and cannot be destroyed. Thus, untruth does not really exist; it is an illusion of 3-D reality.

* Your higher self is your highest, purest connection to Creation. This connection reveals/dissolves all untruths.

* The thing that prevents **Creator Connection** is your **unhealed me**, preventing the "**we**." "We" aligns your perception with **truth as the Creator**; this strengthens and restores the emotional, mental, and physical bodies.

* Creator Connection is made possible because you are love and lovable; your love clears and cleanses all things

that are not love, allowing the raising of your frequency and consciousness. Then you can embrace your waiting divine perfected higher self.

* All of the above creates an **attitude of gratitude**, which is often hidden but never lost. This gratitude supports further direct Creator Communication.

* Gratitude also facilitates healing through the increased vibrations that heal the 3-D bodies through direct energetic/spirit connection.

* Gratitude praises Creation through you while bypassing physical symptoms by connecting with the energetic cause and effect, which shifts your consciousness.

* Being connected to your Creator (you) creates the gift of forgiveness, and being forgiven. This creates an inter-locking network of events that travels throughout your planet, solar system, galaxy, and universe.

* You learn the reason you create dis-ease and so-called death through your Creator Connection; it's all a learn-ing process.

* Creation Connection through your higher self allows you to see the unseen.

* The Laws of Eternity are revealed through Creator Connection, not 3-D time and distance.

* A mighty awareness of Creator Connection is the wisdom that you are all in service to self, one another, your world, and the universe.

* Creator Connection transcends the seen world, allowing the healing of it.

* The balance and importance of giving and receiving are revealed through Creator Connection. Through balance you are strengthening the giver while also supplying strength to the receiver.

* The purpose of time is to allow you to connect with your higher self, the Creator; time will stop when you no longer need to learn from it.

* Eternal truth is revealed to you through Creator Connection, rather than through your often-untruthful mind that believes.

* Creator Connection undoes the past, present, and the future in order to release the now.

* The energetic/spiritual is created through Creator Connection; your thoughts create the physical.

* Meditation and prayer are the means to the Creator Communication; love is received and expressed.

* Creator Communication is an exchange of all love expression, which brings more love to the giver and receiver.

* Creator Communication is your divine right and destiny; it is your natural state of being.

* Creator Communication means you are the Creator expressing itself in all ways all the time.

* You are being taught through Creator Communications that the Creator is all that matters; matter only matters in matter.

Now, dear ones, remember that your higher self already knows all this. Are you ready to apply it and free yourselves from yourselves, and join us in oneness?

WONDERS EXIST EVERYWHERE

There are seen and unseen worlds.
And whether you believe this or not, does not matter.
What matters is for you to know

Wonders exist everywhere,
Whether you know or believe it, or not.

Probabilities and possibilities
Live in the unknown
And when we can surrender to them
They become our own.

The Creator wishes to remind you,
All things are possible
Through knowing your divinity
Which is, by the way,
Always within your vicinity.

The more we embrace and love
Our divinity
The sooner the wonder appears from eternity
And becomes your certainty, for sure.

CHAPTER 55

SO-CALLED DEATH

From the Council of Archangelic Realms (CAR)

Dear Beloved Humans learning to escape incarnational cycles,

The last hurdle of humanity is to learn to escape what you call death; knowing even now there is no such thing as death, you simply transform yourselves from the physical back to the energetic. You are eternal beings of light that never can die, since you are a reflection of Creation itself. All Creation knows how to be and do is to eternally grow and expand—and that's you, dear ones.

Let us briefly discuss where you are in relationship with *death* at the present. Know, dear ones, within your present consciousness and cycle of reality, no soul leaves its physical body one moment before its divine soul plan is complete. This applies to an infant who is within your frequency for just a moment and those who choose to live into what you call old age.

You humans are learning to live your lives within the **Universal Laws of Love**, learning how to fully love self and others. You have not mastered this yet. The sooner you do master the Laws of Love, the easier and more graceful your lives will become. You will learn to create communities of equality, harmony, and balance while honoring one another and your home planet. Those who choose not to love are not going to enjoy the continued consequences of not loving.

When you learn to love, you will release yourselves from the karmic wheel of birth and death, and all problems of human existence will disappear.

While you are still in process with the experience of physical death, let us further discuss what you are experiencing. It is essential that you feel the grief and loss of a loved one during so-called death. Deeply feel the feeling, dear ones, in order to release them from your cellular memory DNA. Also focus on the greater good and journey of the lost loved one. You do not wish to do anything to impede this soul from moving into greater joy and perfection. Try not to make it about yourself.

The God-consciousness within you cannot and does not grieve. This awareness knows and is showing you that everyone is an essential part of the universe and cannot ever leave it. It is your destiny to evolve into ever-increased positive levels of beingness. Through the love force, you can never not exist and must be somewhere, always being drawn to love.

In true divine love there is no such thing as the separation you currently experience; that which feels a sense of separation cannot be love. Love is always functioning through your individual consciousness.

Dear ones, when you think of or feel a loved one who has made his/her transition back into spirit, you are really with that loved one in his/her higher emotions and mental bodies; in effect, your consciousness has merged.

If you can understand the truth shared here, you can lift the chains, which cause useless suffering. Not completely understanding physical to energetic transition is due to the fact that your personality/feeling or belief accepts the body as being the individual, instead of knowing the body is only a garment, which the individual wears temporarily.

Dear ones, when you truly love another, you wish for the other to be happy and harmonious. Can you accept with compassion, thus forgive that your loved one is going on to greater ease and freedom?

When you master the Laws of Love, you will no longer need your cycle of birth and death. You will be eternally free to be just love!

WHY WE DIE

Within our inner being
A life stream flows
Through our physical body.
This stream is a gift from above.
Like water in a stream,
This life stream runs through our pineal,
As no menial task filling our nerves.

The nerves beat our heart,
And that gets everything started.
This permits walking and talking,
And chalking it all up to
The energizing light, often called,
The silver cord,
The accounts and accords the life, we know.

At so-called death,
This silver cord cuts,
And the stream of life,
Stops in its tracks,
And the body stops, as well.

But the real reason things finally stop,
Is due to the waste of life energy,
Through uncontrolled feelings and thoughts
That cause, not so oddly, the disintegration of all our bodies.

The life stream simply slips away,
From the top of the head,
With the silver cord cut,
We are really dead,
As the heart finally ceases to beat,
And we are complete in that lifetime.

ABOUT THE AUTHOR

A Sense of Self: Soul Plan Activation

For over three decades I worked with many very talented and successful people in the advertising and commercial film industries. At the end of my working life, I thought I would morph into quiet. I had begun my advertising career in the heady Man Power/Mad. Ave./mad men days of advertising in the early 1970s, at the top of the ad game at Young & Rubicam, 285 Madison Avenue, New York City. Y&R had the most prestigious accounts, creativity, and billing. It was a great place to work if your family could afford to send you there (their low starting salaries reflected their competitive entry value). Beyond the three-martini and cigarette-smoke-haze lunches, I would find my sense of self.

After a few restless years, in which I changed departments four times (media to sales promotion to account management to creative), Y&R and I finally realized the advertising agency life was not in my divine soul plan. I enrolled in New York University's film school and jumped to the other side of the advertising business: commercial film production. The ad agencies became my clients. My soul plan now linked me with some of the most gifted commercial and feature-film directors in the world—the likes of Ridley and Tony Scott and George Lucas.

The Scott brothers and I, along with many other film people, founded Fairbanks Films, and that company took over the commercial film production advertising world in short order. We produced for Apple Computer founder, Steve Jobs, the famous 1984 TV spot that launched personal cyber technology into the world. Today, this commercial is still considered the most successful TV spot ever created. Mr. Jobs, I know you are still proud, wherever you are, since you put your job on the line for this production. Then the Lucasfilm people decided they wanted to get into the advertising game and came knocking. Why not? After the film industry, the advertising business is one of the most influential and lucrative forms of communication.

So over to Lucasfilm I went, with all their inventive digital technology. It's fair to say, their division of Industrial Light and Magic taught the advertising world digital wizardry, even though others jumped on quickly. It was great fun being the director of marketing of the commercial division, teaching the ad world how to bring any image to the screen (without killing anyone) if they had enough money and time. We changed commercial film forever, producing thousands of spots shown worldwide. Many of these short films became household icons.

During my three decades in advertising and commercial film production, I got to know the planet up close and personal. It was more than anyone could ask of a career! So I thought when it came time to leave it, I surely would be ready for a more peaceful and quieter lifestyle. Wrong!

If you are in the film production business, you get to know California really well. At least I thought I did. The weather, locations, studios, and crews made California an alternative on any production schedule. Only strikes or clients with low budgets would prevent you from shooting in California. Fairbanks Films was my finishing school in Southern California, and the Lucasfilm organization provided my Northern California training. George Lucas preferred Northern California to the south, not resonating with Hollywood values.

While commuting to Northern California from my New York City office for Industrial Light and Magic commercials or Lucasfilm, I often took time to explore wonders the west has to offer. One of my most memorable trips was driving near the top of Mount Shasta, just south of the Oregon border. Mount Shasta is part of the Cascade Mountains, a dramatic volcanic mountain range that snakes its way north into Washington State. The size and grandeur of this mother of mountains was amazing; you could see it from a hundred miles away. We have nothing like it on the East Coast. And I thought enjoying its wondrous size and beauty was enough at the time. I would later learn otherwise. Ten years later, I would return, "awakened" for another purpose entirely.

Some say, as we grow older and get closer to leaving this world, some of us become more spiritually conscious, closer to God Power; women become more masculine and men more feminine, or something like that. Well, anyway, after some medical mishaps and the "enough is enough" syndrome, I did leave the film and advertising businesses.

I mean, what else was I going to do, produce another commercial? The last spot we did was the biggest commercial ever created. It was for Ford Motor Company; ninety days of shooting all over the world, the largest advertising budget ever, and aired around the glove. This was my perfect swan song. Did I need another cue to exit? No! And there was this curious notion that something inside me was yearning to express a new sense of self. Something else was next, but I had no idea what it was. Surrendering to the unknown really challenged my mind, which always had to know.

My mother was of Native American descent and my father was Irish. My father's Celtic grandmother, my great-grandmother, was a backwoods Alabama healer. I call it my "I and I" links (Irish and Indian, both known for native healing). I remember sitting by my great-grandmother's bedside as a young child, listening to her stories of her healing potions and how people would walk for days to get to her for a "healing." She knew how to pick herbs from the forest floor and turn pine-tree sap into a soothing medicine. So I imagined this ability was also in my DNA. It was.

Filmmakers are often multifaceted people. Once, while working with one of my film directors on a project, I developed a cold and shared my family's healing background. My film director friend immediately suggested that I see his alternative medicine doctor, Dr. Herbert Fill. This particular director knew I was at the end of my film career and there was more to cure than a cold. Dr. Fill was a rare mix of psychiatrist, acupuncturist, and homeopath. He had been a commissioner of mental health for the City of New York—working from a Park Avenue office that he ran by himself. It was not long before the patient became a student of alternative medicine under Dr. Fill. This was my transition from advertising into the "healing arts."

Once my transition—or should I say, my transformation—began, it went fairly quickly. After a couple of years of studying under Dr. Fill, I easily moved into training for Reiki, the energy therapy, and light ascension, and became certified in these. These new alternative medical worlds introduced me to an entirely new community of people not associated with advertising or film. I began to know this was not going to be the beginning of a quiet retirement, but a reinvention of myself through a broader use of all my talents and gifts.

My next transition took me into other higher-realm dimensions, not unlike the worlds George Lucas brought to the silver screen. Maybe that's the reason my career included the Lucas organization—to better prepare me for what was to come. Anyhow, what transpired next felt organic, extraordinary, and natural at the same time. And I realized many of George Lucas's stories were real.

The next destination/stop on my transformation train took me on a sacred journey to Egypt, where I connected with higher beings in the King's Chamber of the Great Pyramid. Later, I considered working with *New York Times* best-selling author Neale Donald Walsch of the *Conversations with God* books, and began to connect with higher beings myself. If George Lucas could imagine other worlds that gave us hope, and people like Neale Donald Walsh could communicate with God, why couldn't I do something similar?

As I was often enthralled by divine messengers (God, archangels, galaxy and star beings), could I listen to the message, apply it, and see if it could improve my life or the lives of others?

Yes, I could! Today, there are millions of people worldwide who connect with multiple dimensions through cyberspace, books, films, workshops, or by directly experiencing messages from other realms. Can we accept wisdom from sources other than the human mind? That is the question of the day. The number of people connecting beyond the human mind seems to be increasing daily. Something is shifting, not only in me but in the world. We are beginning to realize that we are not alone; that our planet, our galaxy, and the universe are more diverse than we ever imagined, and there is a plan in it all. And we need the help of those other realms if we are to grow and evolve in a healthy way.

Through years of personal processing work and working with others who were already "connecting," I began to trust and know that ours was not the only frequency/dimension in existence (Einstein and string theory physicists had already suggested this). Now I would begin to connect with these higher frequencies myself, along with many others. OK, I want to be the first to acknowledge this is the tricky part for some. I, too, come from a world that says, "If you cannot show me or prove it, it does not exist." Some people simply will not be able to accept or believe my story from this point on. For those who know the truth, that's cool, a gift. For those who cannot accept what is being said, or see it simply as fiction or untrue, that's OK. The mind believes; the heart knows. But try to apply the message, if it resonates.

Ten years after my first journey to Mount Shasta, I returned there as a transformed guy with a lot of hard-core business experience behind me. I joined other like-minded/spirited people on a sacred journey back to Mount Shasta. Little did

I know ten years earlier that it is considered one of the most powerful spiritual portals on Earth. We were there to serve as proxies for humanity, performing specific rituals on the mountain to assist the planet and all of us to move into higher levels of consciousness through a unique opportunity called ascension—a consciousness of being at one with all that is.

On our journey, we would heal some wounded aspects within ourselves, which allowed us to connect with a higher-dimensional civilization inside the planet that coexists with us and intends for us to join together with it in the future. Where was George Lucas now?

Later, I would cofound a website, www.theangelnewsnetwork.com, and a metaphysical school to teach and share what I had learned. I began connecting with other like-minded/ spirited people, writing and connecting more with various higher realms. Each day, I sense I am always at the beginning of an ever-growing process of a sense of self and an expanding universe.

So when you get ready for a life change, watch out! You never know what destiny (your soul plan) may have in store for you. You just might end up talking to angels and all sorts of higher-realm beings that may change you and your world. *Activate Your Soul Plan!* is a testament to that truth.

Phillip Elton Collins is a teacher, healing arts therapist, conscious channel, ex-journalist, ad man, author/poet, and cofounder of the Angel News Network in Fort Lauderdale, New York City, and Los Angeles, and the Modern Day Mystery School. His other books include: *Coming Home to Lemuria: An Ascension Adventure Story* (being adapted into a stage play and screenplay), *Sacred Poetry and Mystical Messages: To Change Your*

Life and the World (116 original poems and twenty Inner Earth messages), *Man Power God Power* (a volume of higher-realm teachings), and *The Happiness Handbook: Being Present Is the Present (Phrases of Presence to Set Us Free to Be...Happy).* All his books present the author's soul plan activation.

RESOURCES

The Angel News Network
www.theangelnewsnetwork.com

Phillip Elton Collins
www.facebook.com/PhillipEltonCollins
Coming Home to Lemuria: An Ascension Adventure Story
Order via: http://theangelnewsnetwork.com/page22/book-coming-Home.html
The Happiness Handbook: Being Present Is the Present (Phrases of Presence to Set Us Free to Be...Happy)
Order via: http://theangelnewsnetwork.com/book-happiness-handbook.html
Sacred Poetry and Mystical Messages: To Change Your Life and the World
Order via: http://www.theangelnewsnetwork.com/book-sacred-poetry.html
Man Power God Power
Order via: http://theangelnewsnetwork.com/book_man-power-god-power.html

Joel D. Anastasi

The Ascension Handbook

www.facebook.com/TheAscensionHandbookCreate
YourEcstaticUnionWithGod

Order via: http://www.theangelnewsnetwork.com/ascension_
handbook.html

Life Mastery

https://www.facebook.com/TheLifeMasteryProgram

Order via: http://www.theangelnewsnetwork.com/book-life-
mastery.html

The Second Coming: The Archangel Gabriel Proclaims a New Age

www.gabrielsecondcoming.com

www.facebook.com/GabrielTheSecondComing

Order via: http://www.theangelnewsnetwork.com/book-second-
coming.html

Jeff Fasano and Jeff Fasano Photography

www.jefffasano.com

www.facebook.com/JeffFasanoPhotography

Journey of the Awakened Heart

www.journeyoftheawakenedheart.net

www.facebook.com/Journeyoftheawakenedheart

Order via: http://theangelnewsnetwork.com/page23/book-
journey.html

BACK COVER COPY

Did you know you come fully equipped with a divine soul plan (your purpose in being here) each lifetime? It is up to you to choose to activate it through your freedom of choice and will.

This book is filled with tools to teach you how to activate your soul plan. There are *angel answers and actions* throughout this endeavor to support your *call to action*, giving you a foundation like never before to know who you are and why you are here.

The activation of your soul plan will set you free from all that has kept you in lack and limitation. The guidance here is *portals of universal wisdoms* to assist you in creating a loving relationship with self and in creating communities of equality, harmony, and balance.

We are the spokes off the hub of the wheel that the universe rides upon. Through your soul plan expressed it will become the fuel to power this wheel, allowing each spoke of the wheel to be your soul plan activation.

Whether you believe angels exist and we can talk to them does not matter. What matters is the love and support contained in the information received. Can humanity begin to accept we are advancing as a species due to forces beyond our mind or sometimes comprehension at this time?

Open this book at any random chapter and see what your soul plan can receive right now. If you are ready to receive a major divine *download* of information, dare to read the entire book. The author received these teachings through a rapid upload; what he receives he now gives, balancing giving and receiving.

Phillip Elton Collins is a certified light ascension therapist, an ordained minister, and cofounder of the Angel News Network and the Modern Day Mystery School. He is a teacher, author, poet, channeler of higher realms, and filmmaker who addresses the integration of the emotional, mental, and physical bodies. He was the director of marketing for George Lucas's Industrial Light and Magic commercials, a founder of Fairbanks Films International with directors Ridley and Tony Scott, and gained extensive corporate advertising experience at Young & Rubicam in New York.

Previous books:

The Happiness Handbook: Being Present Is the Present (Phrases of Presence to Set Us Free to Be...Happy)

Man Power God Power

Sacred Poetry and Mystical Messages: To Change Your Life and the World

Coming Home to Lemuria: An Ascension Adventure Story

49023344R00221

Made in the USA
Columbia, SC
18 January 2019